JESUS, LIFE COACH

LEARN FROM THE BEST

LAURIE BETH JONES

OLIVER
NELSON
™

NELSON BUSINESS
A Division of Thomas Nelson Publishers
Since 1798

www.thomasnelson.com

Published in Nashville, Tennessee, by Thomas Nelson, Inc.

Nelson Business books may be purchased in bulk for educational, business, fundraising, or sales promotional use. For information, please email SpecialMarkets@ThomasNelson.com.

Unless otherwise noted, Scripture quotations are from the KING JAMES VERSION.

Scripture quotations noted NJB are from the NEW JERUSALEM BIBLE, Doubleday, 1999.

Scripture quotations noted *The Message* are from *The Message: The New Testament in Contemporary English*. Copyright © 1993 by Eugene H. Peterson.

Scripture quotations noted NRSV are from the NEW REVISED STANDARD VERSION of the Bible. Copyright © 1989 by the Division of Christian Education of the National Council of Churches of Christ in the U.S.A. All rights reserved.

Scripture quotations noted NKJV are from THE NEW KING JAMES VERSION. Copyright © 1982 by Thomas Nelson, Inc. Used by permission. All rights reserved.

Scripture quotations noted NLT are from the *Holy Bible*, New Living Translation, copyright © 1996. Used by permission of Tyndale House Publishers, Inc., Wheaton, Illinois 60189. All rights reserved.

Scripture quotations noted CEV are from THE CONTEMPORARY ENGLISH VERSION. © 1991 by the American Bible Society. Used by permission.

Scripture quotations noted NIV are from the HOLY BIBLE: NEW INTERNATIONAL VERSION. Copyright © 1973, 1978, 1984 by International Bible Society. Used by permission of Zondervan Publishing House. All rights reserved.

Library of Congress Cataloging-in-Publication Data

Jones, Laurie Beth.
    Jesus, life coach : learn from the best / Laurie Beth Jones.
      p. cm.
    ISBN 0-7852-8783-3 (tp)
    ISBN 0-7852-6190-7 (hardcover)
    1. Christian life. 2. Success—Religious aspects—Christianity. I. Title.
BV4598.3.J66 2004
248.4—dc22
                                      2003023394

Printed in the United States of America
07 08 09 10 RRD 5 4

To my mother, Irene A. Jones,
who taught me to paint what I love.

To my DEAR FRIEND KENNY,
WHO I LOVE LIKE A BROTHER.

HOPE YOU ENJOY AS MUCH AS I DID!

LOVE
ALWAYS,

CHRISTINA

DEC/2007

CONTENTS

PRODUCTIVITY   165
WITH JESUS AS YOUR LIFE COACH, YOU WILL . . .

FULFILLMENT

WITH JESUS AS YOUR LIFE COACH, YOU WILL . . .

INTRODUCTION

Whether I am meeting with the president of Wal-Mart or the officers of the U.S. Naval Academy in Annapolis, I know that the one question that is most on their minds is this: How can I coach others towards their highest and best?

After spending a lifetime studying the character of Jesus, and the better part of my career working with leaders, I have come to this conclusion. There is no better role model for coaching that gets lasting results than Jesus of Nazareth. This book is my contribution towards the profound gift and skill set known as coaching.

Coaching is definitely "in." Whereas at one time only athletes had coaches, now everyone from CEOs to at-risk youth is becoming familiar with the term *coach*. The International Coaching Federation, which began with a handful of people, now has more than five thousand members. It seems that nearly everyone these days either has a coach or wants one.

Currently more than 150,000 people worldwide call themselves life coaches, and more are being added to that number every day. Therapists as well as corporate trainers are flocking to this newfound profession and enjoying it. As one therapist stated in an article on coaching in the July-August 2002 issue of *Psychotherapy Networker*, "Therapy, for me, was focused on looking backward into why I was the way I was. Coaching looks at where you are today, where you want to go, and how you're going to get there." In that same article Coach Harriett Salinger said, "I think people know what they want. What they need are arms to hold them as they make the discovery."

Another contributor to that article was reporter Jim Nauton, who wrote, "The ever more challenging character of modern life has created a market for men and women that can provide, for a fee, a service that older generations once performed for younger generations. Since World War II, increased mobility and the decline of family and community ties have reduced intergenerational contact, with the result that a lot of the support structures in people's lives have broken down."

While Nauton wrote that "the coach's role expands from framing issues in revealing ways to serving as goad and cheerleader," organizational development guru Peter Drucker asserted that the coach's role is to "help people find their strengths, and build on them."

My friend and coaching client Jane Creswell shared with me a research paper presented at the Executive Coaching Summit convened at a recent International Coaching Federation conference. A group of experts decided that all coaches "should have proficiencies in listening, creating an environment for change, facilitating self-awareness, and should be able to work with personal, professional, and perhaps organizational issues about which their clients want to focus." Paper authors Dr. Lee Smith and Dr. Jeannine Sandstrom further noted that "executive coaching is a facilitative one-to-one, mutually designed relationship which exists . . . for the benefit of a client who is accountable for highly complex decisions."

A good executive coaching interaction should include such elements as "the ability to be fully present, conscious and spontaneous, the ability to ask powerful questions, be a direct communicator, and raise the client's awareness." An advanced coach would also "hold a high level of confidence, challenge people at high levels, speak the truth and the secrets when no one else will. They also must be a confidante, which allows adults to share all sides of themselves; their hopes as well as fears, their wants as well as their needs; their dreams for themselves as well as for their organizations."

An article in the *Boston Globe* (March 16, 2003) by Diane E. Lewis reported that an increasing number of Fortune 500 companies are hiring coaches to make sure that executives survive the critical first ninety to one hundred days of their new employment. Such companies as Fidelity Investments, Johnson & Johnson, State Farm Insurance, and Cisco Systems are working diligently on assimilating or "onboarding" coaching practices. The goal is to help business leaders increase retention levels as well as adjust to new jobs faster.

Lewis wrote that scandals on Wall Street have made

companies painfully aware that mismatched or unhappy employees can lead to corrosion and corruption in companies in addition to lost profits and productivity. Further, a study commissioned by a Chicago outplacement firm stated that executives left U.S. firms in "unprecedented numbers" in the last three years.

In 1999, when outplacement firm Challenger, Gray and Christmas first began tracking the exodus of CEOs, only thirty-two resigned or were forced out during that year. Today, according to the article, chief executives step down at an average of seventy-nine per month.

A study commissioned by a Fortune 500 firm through MetrixGlobal, LLC determined that executive coaching produced an astounding 529 percent return on investment. Seventy-five percent of the participants indicated that coaching had significant or very significant impact on at least one of nine business measures. Sixty percent of the respondents were able to identify specific financial benefits that came as a result of their coaching.

Overall, productivity (60 percent favorable) and employee satisfaction (54 percent) were cited as most significantly impacted by coaching. Work quality and work output were stated to be significantly impacted by the executive coaching program. Executive Coaches Jane Creswell and Jerry Fletcher asserted that coaching helps identify "High Performance Patterns" in individuals on teams, and thus leverage the truest asset of any organization, which is knowledge.

Coaching is getting the attention of church leaders, too. Director of the Hollifield Leadership Center George Bullard wrote in the September 2002 issue of *NETResults* magazine:

> Coaching is an emerging right brained approach that sees relationship as more important than tasks, significance as more important than success, stories as more important than strategies, experiences as more important than rule books, people as more important than institutions, soaring with strengths as more important than "problem solving."

As I looked at the research on coaching assembled before me, I was struck by how qualified and how perfect Jesus is as a Life Coach. And as if my attention surrounding coaching was a magnet, I suddenly began receiving multiple e-mail requests a day, asking me to develop a faith-based coaching program that had Jesus as the model.

In our time together here I am going to share with you thoughts, reflections, observations, stories, and personal experiences of what it is like to have Jesus as a personal Coach. But first I want to give you a little background.

My life with Jesus as my personal Coach began officially when I was fourteen. My asking him to come into my heart and be my Lord and Savior was an accumulation of events and experiences, such as hymns sung around the organ with my grandparents and many hours sitting on pews in Presbyterian and Methodist churches with my father, mother, sister, and brother.

One summer before my freshman year in high school I went on a trip with my best friend, Nancy. Our parents let us take a train ride to Mexico City to meet a family there who would entertain us and show us the town. On the way there we spent the night at a small hacienda, owned by friends of Nancy's parents. After the couple met us at the train and took us out for lunch, each of us retired to a separate room. After unpacking my bag, I walked into the courtyard that overlooked the valley below. It was late afternoon in a hot July. From a distance I could see the workers from the local mine making their way up the hill toward home. There were thunderclouds building on the horizon, and a mockingbird was singing in the tree behind me. Suddenly I experienced "awe." It was transcendent—an almost out-of-body, yet very much in-the-world experience. For the moment it felt like I was both the bird and the note the bird was singing. Like I was the line of men climbing the hill, as well as the sky vaulting over them. It was as if I was everywhere at once, and the entire experience was suffused with both a profound knowing and an all-encompassing love. In that moment I knew that God was real, and *I* was real. I breathed a silent prayer as I leaned into the adobe wall, asking Jesus to come into my life and guide me—as Teacher, Friend, Lover, and lifelong personal Coach.

In that moment Jesus went from being a figure on a cross to a Friend walking alongside me. We have since laughed together, cried together, not spoken for months at a time, argued over principles, and danced in sunlit meadows. I have seen him leaning up against a stone column in a bookstore, smiling and waiting to take me home after a long day of book signing.

I have sat with him in airports, just watching the people, asking him what he was thinking about when he created this person or that one. I have sat silent with him at my father's funeral, shocked at the sudden loss of my driving force. I have put my last hundred dollars into the offering plate at church, not knowing how I was going to pay the rent, and laughed in awe as money started flowing to me in an ever-increasing amount. It has been the most challenging, exhilarating, fear-filled, exasperating, and wonderful relationship in my life. I would not want to be without him for anything.

In preparing for this book I read again the psalms of King David—struck anew by the passionately personal relationship this individual had with God. Whether he was praising God for the beauty of the night sky or pleading with him to lift him out of the depths of despair, David knew that God *knew* him and had a keen interest in every aspect of his waking life. He wrote,

> The LORD is my shepherd;
> I shall not want.

He maketh me to lie down in green pastures . . .

He restoreth my soul: he leadeth me in the paths of
    righteousness for his name's sake.

Yea, though I walk through the valley of the shadow of
    death . . .

thy rod and thy staff they comfort me.

Thou preparest a table before me in the presence of mine
    enemies . . .

Surely goodness and mercy shall follow me all the days
    of my life:

and I will dwell in the house of the LORD for ever.

(Ps. 23)

What beautiful imagery of a person and his God, his
Coach, if you will, comforting and guiding him with rod
and staff, walking alongside him in the valley of darkness,
ensuring him that he had a future even when he was in the
presence of his enemies, restoring his soul. Who wouldn't
want a Coach like that?

Being invited to speak in venues ranging from Fortune
500 retreats to international conferences has been a challenge and an honor. At these events I am sometimes pri-
vately asked to explain the basis for my Christianity. A
speaker approached me one year and said, "I believe that
God is pure being. Yet I sense in you a calmness and cen-
teredness that I don't have. What is it?"

I smiled and told him, "I believe that God is pure being,

too, Richard, but I know that God also knows my middle name and watches with great interest and love everything that I do. While you believe in God, I know that God believes in me."

He smiled and said, "I want that."

I smiled back and said, "All you need to do is ask."

It is an honor and a challenge to write about Jesus as a personal Coach because it speaks to me of the richest and most rewarding relationship possible on this earth. But before we go any further, I need to ask the question that has permeated the ages: What do *you* think about Jesus? Who do you think he is?

Jesus is one of the most revered and misrepresented figures in history. His life has inspired saints and incited riots. His image, which we have only reconstructed since there were no cameras in his time, decorates and sanctifies some of the most beautiful buildings in the world. His name is used for both cursing and blessing. Some people who sing it in churches on Sunday are afraid to mention it at work on Monday. People who claim to be his representatives have committed some of the most heinous acts against humanity. Religions have sprung up around him, nations have been divided, cultures have been delineated, and families have been torn apart. Clearly this man has had an impact on history.

When I spoke at the International Conference on Business and Spirituality held in Acapulco, Mexico, I asked the 350 people assembled in the ballroom, "How many of you come from a Judeo-Christian background?" Nearly 80 percent of the people raised a hand. I then asked, "How many of you have been hurt or turned away from your religion because of ill-informed people who used religion to try to do you harm?" Virtually the same number of hands went up.

I shared with them that religious representatives had wounded me too. Yet I was there to address spirituality, not religion, and relationship, not doctrine. I asked them to bow their heads with me in prayer, and I asked God to heal any wounds and hurts that they had suffered at the hands of misinformed representatives. I also asked that I would never be one of those people. As I finished the prayer, the group seemed to heave a collective sigh of relief. When their heads came up, I could sense that their hearts were open.

I'm going to ask you to do the same thing. For a moment, let's just ask for healing for any of the hurts inflicted on you in the name of religion. Let's also ask forgiveness for those who, through malice or ignorance, may have hurt you.

The words and observations I'm about to share with you now are not about religion, but about relationship. I have at times been met with astonishment when I remind people that Jesus was not a Christian (nor was Mary a Catholic). It is the man-made dogmas of religions that have divided and alienated us from our true core, which is love.

Each of us is made in the image of God, and to God we will return. But what about in the meantime? What is this thing called life, and how are we to live it to the fullest?

Jesus gave us his mission statement when he said, "I have come that you might have life, and have it abundantly" (my paraphrase of John 10:10). Just for a moment repeat those words, adding your name in the sentence as if Jesus was talking to you. In my case it would be, "Laurie Beth, I have come that you might have life, and have it abundantly."

I do not believe that we can or should harness God in order to make more money. The profound truth, which continues to elude so many of us, is that when we allow God to harness *us*, we become fulfilled. And fulfillment is the ultimate success, is it not?

With my first book *Jesus, CEO: Using Ancient Wisdom for Visionary Leadership*, I asked corporate leaders to consider a man who had only three years to train twelve people, none of whom was divine. Yet in that time he managed to turn a diverse, at times cowardly and contentious, group into "lean, clean marketing machines." He trained them so well that they were willing to work for no pay and die for him. That book has become an international bestseller, translated into twelve foreign languages. The universality of these principles appeals to people from different walks of life, especially those who are leading the ones who are working in business.

When I asked corporate leaders how many of them would like to have a staff like that, nearly all of them raised their hands. When I said, "Well, the catch is that you have to go first," nearly all of the hands went down. They began to realize that Jesus was less about success and more about transformation. And to many, that is a frightening process.

Because you have purchased this book, I trust that you are willing and wanting to make changes in your life—changes for the better. Everywhere Jesus went he orchestrated change—whether it was turning a withered hand into a whole one, or a frightened woman into a bold proclaimer of truth.

When he told his apostles, "Go and tell everyone what you have seen and heard," he wasn't telling them to bonk people on the head with their (as yet nonexistent) Bibles and convert them to think as they did. He was calling them to testify to the transformed lives they had seen . . . how blind people could see, how lame people could walk, how mute people could speak, how those who were covered in ashes of despair wore a garland of hope instead.

That same power—that same divine desire for wholeness and healing—is still at work today . . . waiting merely to be called upon, listened to, and believed.

In this book, which is divided into four sections, I will show how Jesus will help you gain focus, balance, productivity, and fulfillment. Since I believe the groundwork for any coaching process is having the person first establish a mission, I ask you to write your mission or life purpose in a single sentence. I cover this extensively in my second book, *The Path: Creating Your Mission for Work and Life*, offering a number of key principles and exercises designed to help people and organizations do this. I won't repeat those processes here. But if you do not have a mission, get one. That is the prerequisite, I believe, for beginning this work.

Until we *focus* and define what is most important to us, we live our lives in a haze of other-directed urgencies. Coaching is designed to help you stay focused—to practice "planned abandonment" of opportunities that would merely serve as distractions. You will be taught to use your sword—and gladly—as well as ask open-ended questions that keep your eyes on the prize.

Without *balance*, the best gains become burdens, and losses can pull us under. With Jesus as your Coach, you will understand how to strike and maintain a sense of balance in a world that careens and teeters on the edges of our ever shifting desires. You will no longer feel a need to justify your behaviors, and you will develop a new respect for your fragile things. You will understand the difference between archetypes and stereotypes, and learn that a rough start is better than no start at all.

Productivity is the goal of every leader, manager, and coach. We must learn how to think inside the solution in order to bear fruit and remain alive with constantly expanding new possibilities. You will learn how to avoid "borrowed armor." Swimming upstream will become your goal, rather than something you avoid, and outrageous requests will become your daily fare.

Fulfillment is beyond "success." Knowing the difference will determine what roads and what actions you choose to take throughout the day. The shift of a few inches either way can make all the difference. With Jesus as your Coach, you will begin to experience unbounded joy in his presence, no matter what. You will become more of a voice, rather than an echo, and daily begin to paint what you love. You will have new stories to tell as well as a renewed self-image. You will learn to be comfortable in a future state.

Research conducted by Harvard researcher Gerald Zaltman in his book *What Customers Think* revealed that we want people and organizations who will

- ✦ save us time,

- ✦ be a resource for new ideas,

- ✦ connect with us relationally, and

- ✦ stay with us on the journey, through all its twists and turns.

Jesus is that person.
Welcome to your new Life Coach.

FOCUS

My friend Joe Mathews shared a poignant story with me recently. His best friend's wife was diagnosed with terminal cancer and given a short time to live. Joe said he watched in awe as Dan and his wife, Christine, began to live each day with tremendous clarity and love. When it was nearly the end Joe finally got up the courage to ask Christine the question: "What does it feel like to live each day knowing you are dying?" She raised herself up on one arm, and then asked him, "Joe, what does it feel like to live each day pretending that you are not?"

One of the most powerful questions for focusing is asking yourself: "What would I be doing with my time if I knew I had only six healthy months to live?" It can immediately cause you to reorganize your priorities.

Focus is the beginning of power.

Last year I spoke on the phone with a client that I have been coaching. A highly successful entrepreneur, he had a vague idea of what he wanted and needed to do next in his life to take him to a higher level. He said he had read *The Path* but had not written down his answers to the questions. For his first assignment I had him go back and write down the answers to the questions. In writing his vision specifically, he got very clear about what he wanted to create and experience in his life.

I ran into him recently, and he was laughing exultantly. Everything he had written in his vision since our first discussion had come true—not in three years, but in ninety days. He said, "As soon as I got clear about the 'vision thing'— *wham!* Everything started coming to me so quickly. Now you need to write the next book to tell me what to do when all of my vision starts coming true all at once." We laughed about the dilemma of the fishermen who followed Jesus' instructions to throw the net on the other side of the boat and hauled in such a catch of fish that it threatened to overwhelm their vessel.

Such a catch of fish is waiting for you, too. Are you ready?

When Jesus, your personal Coach, looks at you, he will ask you one question: "What do you want me to do for you?" That was the question he asked again and again in his ministry—whether it was a Roman soldier, anxious about the failing health of his favorite assistant, or a woman who had been suffering a hemorrhage for twelve years. "What do you want me to do for you?"

Jesus is asking you to focus now. All the power is here. All the goodwill is here. All the intent is here right now.

It is up to you to decide on who you want to be and what you want to be about in this world.

The following chapters are designed to help you focus—to help you go from being a lightbulb, illuminating a small space, to a laser beam, powerful enough to cut through steel.

HAVE YOUR
TENT STOLEN

NOW WE SEE ONLY REFLECTIONS IN
A MIRROR . . . BUT THEN WE SHALL
BE SEEING FACE TO FACE.
—1 CORINTHIANS 13:12 (NJB)

Recently I had the pleasure of hearing Ray Anderson, founder of a textile mill in Georgia named Interface, speak to a group of business leaders in Santa Fe. He told the following story.

It seems that one day Sherlock Holmes and his assistant, Watson, went camping. As the night wore on, Sherlock woke up, leaned over, and asked Watson, "What do you see?" Watson responded, "Sherlock, I see the North Star, which has helped guide us to this spot. Beyond that I see the Big Dipper and the tail of Orion. I also can make out the edges of the Milky Way and know that there are universes expanding beyond that."

Watson was about to continue his rapturous explanation when suddenly Sherlock elbowed him and hissed, "Watson, you idiot, someone has stolen our tent!"

Laughter rippled through the audience as the multiple real-life applications of this story became apparent. Watson was rhapsodizing about the beauty of the universe, and Sherlock the detective was concerned with the crime that made their new view possible.

Jesus once described himself as coming "like a thief in the night." I love the idea of his coming to steal our tent—the tent of our limited perspective—the tent of our fragile and segmented understandings—the tent that we think is keeping us safe, but is really just keeping us from seeing the universe.

Like children huddled in a tent, we talk to each other in the light of our little flashlights, considering ourselves bold adventurers—but we haven't even left our own backyard.

I wrote a chapter in *Jesus in Blue Jeans* regarding God's impatience with "stiff necked" people. Stubbornness is first cousin to arrogance, and pride always precedes a fall. When we think that we know it all . . . when we refuse to try another way of doing things . . . when we are determined to remain inflexible and ignorant, we are doomed to failure.

Some time ago I hosted a birthday party for a friend. When one of the invited guests arrived, she admitted that she was a little late because she couldn't find her glasses. She laughed and said, "I finally just grabbed the closest pair I could find. I think these are my mother's." We all chuckled as she described how difficult it had been to drive over to the house, looking through lenses that belonged to somebody else.

How often do we just grab our parent's glasses when we head out on a journey, and not use "new eyes" to view the world? I am continuously amazed and chagrined at how often we repeat our parents' negative patterns. It is how a culture is created, I suppose, and how one declines.

If only we would open our eyes to new ways of relating, seeing, and doing. If only we would focus not on the tent that has been stolen, but on our suddenly expanding view of the universe. Watch out, oh you who desire growth.

Jesus will steal your tent.

QUESTIONS

1. Where in life are you using your mother's or father's glasses?

2. How big is your tent?

3. How limiting is it?

4. What is the value of the kind of "thievery" we are talking about in this chapter?

Dear Lord,
Thank you for stealing the tent of my small-mindedness and limited thinking. Help me realize that nothing is lost, but much more is gained, when you steal away my oh so comfortable limitations. Amen.

PRACTICE

PLANNED

ABANDONMENT

MARY HAS CHOSEN THE BETTER PART.
—LUKE 10:42 (NRSV)

Frances Hesselbein is chairman and founding president of the Drucker Foundation, as well as the former CEO of the Girl Scouts of the USA. She began her work as a volunteer troop leader and vowed to defend the core values of the Girl Scouts while recommitting the organization to its mission of "helping girls reach their highest potential."

She determined that any girl in America should be able

to see herself in a Girl Scout uniform—whether she was Navajo or Vietnamese or a young girl in rural America. She also determined that the organization had to become more relevant. Girls were not so in need of preparing for marriage as for math, and had to be prepared not only to work in the kitchen but also to avoid teen pregnancies.

Hesselbein began a relentless crusade to narrow the focus while broadening the reach. During her tenure the Girl Scouts went from a membership of one million girls to more than two million, with 780,000 adult volunteers. Her accomplishments were noticed by none other than Peter Drucker himself, the man many credit as being the father of the modern organization. Drucker recruited Hesselbein to start and run his Drucker Foundation, which is dedicated to helping nonprofit organizations run more efficiently.

Hesselbein calls herself the chief cheerleader of Drucker's principles. One principle that she quotes most frequently in her book *Hesselbein on Leadership* is that of "planned abandonment." She writes, "If we are to remain mission focused, as we must be if we are to be relevant in an uncertain age, then abandoning those things that do not further the mission is a leadership imperative."

Hesselbein is in good company. Jim Collins, author of *Built to Last* and *Good to Great*, writes about Hesselbein. He states that Frances follows three basic tests of mission, understanding that to do good does not mean to do all good. According to Collins, the three basic tests of mission relevance are these: "First, the opportunity must fit squarely in the midst of the organization's mission. Second, the enterprise must have the ability to execute on the opportunity better than any other organization. And third, the opportunity must make sense in the context of the economic engine and resources of the organization."

Planned abandonment means learning how and when to say no, as well as cultivating the discipline of saying no. Because we live in a day and age when opportunities are endless, and "acres of diamonds" lay everywhere at our feet, we need to be able to understand what to pick up and what to put down.

Jesus understood this and demonstrated it when he put down the hammer in the carpenter shop and picked up his walking stick. Being a carpenter was something he did very well, but there was something higher and more unique that he could do better than anyone else. He went toward that "occupation," and the world was forever changed.

Because a theme of my work is finding your divine calling and living it, I counsel people from many walks of life, all endeavoring to reach out and grasp "the high calling of God in Christ Jesus" (Phil. 3:14). Invariably the challenges they face are due not to lack of opportunity but to the multiplicity of choices.

Having too many choices can be just as paralyzing as having few or no choices at all. I have watched a woman surrender her chairmanship of a church board, only to go on to become a congregational coach throughout her region. I have watched a CEO relinquish his opportunity to become president of his national trade association, so he could drill down deeper into the roots of his organization and solidify its growing success. I have watched a speech pathologist turn over her practice to friends and associates, so she could get on with the work of church planting and growth. I have watched a man struggle with the decision about whether to become a lifetime deacon of his church or devote more time to his family. Every decision was an agonizing one because it meant leaving others . . . disappointing others . . . leaving a gap in services. But the decisions were made, and somehow the gaps were filled.

As someone whose mission involves the words *divine connection*, I have had to struggle with decisions that meant loosening ties with others. Whenever I have to make a decision that means leaving someone behind, I am reminded of something. What would I be doing if I had only six healthy months to live? That question always eases and triggers some planned abandonment of projects and tasks that could be done by others. Abandonment to God means abandonment to bliss. And that is worth planning for.

Now, I want to say a word here about false abandonment. Perhaps you are as dubious as I am when I hear of a politician, who has been caught in a scandal or who is losing popularity in the polls, deciding that he wants to return home to "spend more time with his family." That is not a planned choice—that is a default choice because his chosen route isn't open to him anymore. There is a difference.

Planned abandonment doesn't mean walking away from something that is difficult or isn't working anymore. Planned abandonment means choosing between good and great, between better and best. Planned abandonment means that you are able to say no to all that glitters and discern what truly shines. Once you understand the difference, you are on your way to fulfillment.

I love this story:

> As Jesus and his disciples were on their way, he came to a village where a woman named Martha opened her home to him. She had a sister called Mary, who sat at the Lord's feet listening to what he said. But Martha was distracted by all the preparations that had to be made. She came to him and asked, "Lord, don't you care that my sister has left me to do the work by myself? Tell her to help me!"
>
> "Martha, Martha," the Lord answered, "you are worried and upset about many things, but only one thing is needed. Mary has chosen what is better, and it will not be taken away from her." (Luke 10:38–42 NIV)

When Mary chose to leave her kitchen duties in favor of listening to Jesus, she was praised for her planned abandonment. She decided to let lesser things go in order to choose the higher part.

Jesus practiced planned abandonment.

QUESTIONS

1. What opportunities are confusing you right now? Name specific choices you are facing.

2. Which one of those can you do better than almost anyone else?

3. Which one of those fits squarely in line with your personal mission?

4. Which one of those is in context with your economic engine and resources?

5. Why must you and I learn to say no?

Dear Lord,

Jesus could have stayed very busy as a carpenter or even as someone who could turn stones into bread out in the wilderness. He gave up the mundane in order to follow the path that was his alone. Help me to follow the path that is mine alone. Amen.

KEEP YOUR

FOCUS

LET YOUR EYES LOOK STRAIGHT AHEAD,
AND YOUR EYELIDS LOOK RIGHT BEFORE YOU.
—PROVERBS 4:25 (NKJV)

It was early in my career, and I wasn't getting all the hot bookings. I remember distinctly standing by the airport luggage carousel in Minneapolis with my media escort as we watched hundreds of assorted sizes of look-alike luggage roll past us.

I asked him how he got this work, and he said, "Oh, I just fill in now and then. The other folks usually take the big authors and leave the other ones to me." This let me know immediately where I stood in the scheme of things.

We then proceeded to a cable television station that had seen better days. I noticed with interest that some guys in a band were unpacking their drum set in the parking lot, unloading it carefully from a gray van. I thought, *How unusual. I wonder what that is about?*

I then made my way into the station where I was greeted by a woman who turned out to be not only the greeter, but apparently also my interviewer. Not only was she the interviewer, but she was also the camera person. She led me to the studio, sat me down on one of two stools positioned in front of the camera, and said, "My name is Rita. I will ask you a question with the camera turned on me. Then I will get up and turn the camera on you, and you will answer it." I said, "Okay, I can do this," and we began.

It was a bit challenging for me to concentrate when she asked the question, then jumped up and turned the camera on me, even though I had to remain looking at the same spot where she used to be, but was no longer. I was managing this "acting" feat okay until the noise started up in the parking lot. *Bang! Crash! Bang, bang, bing, bing! Crash, crash, crash!* The band, which was to go on next, was practicing in the parking lot.

The thin walls of the station transmitted the noise right into our studio. Rita became disturbed by this—very disturbed. She began making hand motions to me, which were basically indecipherable. I continued to speak about the main points in my book somehow, yet found it even more challenging to look straight ahead and *keep* talking when she got off the stool, crawled past me on the floor, ran out the door, and yelled, "Shut up!" at the top of her lungs. All the while I was talking into the camera about my book. She then came back, crawled past me again, and sat back on the stool, reaching around to turn the camera to her as if nothing had happened. On book tours, as in life, you must learn to stay focused, no matter what is happening around you.

I have a friend who is basically what you might call a Diet Coke fan (*addict* might be a better word). You will seldom, if ever, see her without a Diet Coke in her hand. The other day we were leaving a meeting and she somehow tripped over a broken sidewalk. Almost in slow motion I saw her lunge forward, tilt backward, twist to avoid hitting a child walking past her, lurch two steps forward, and then recover herself. All the while the Diet Coke can in her hand never moved. It was proof to me that what she valued almost more than her dignity, her safety, or her personal well-being was that Diet Coke.

There is a point of focus in your life that is like that Diet Coke can, isn't there? No matter what else is going on around you, you will somehow manage to make sure that it remains undisturbed. What is it?

No matter what was going on in Jesus' life, he kept his focus. It never wavered. Whether people were praising him with palm fronds or whipping him with cords, his focus remained the same.

He came to do the will of his Father, no matter what. Whether he was at a party or a funeral, a meeting or a prayer breakfast, he always stayed true to what he came here to do.

When I was given the incredible gift of a ten-day trip to the Holy Land, it seemed as if my mind could not enlarge itself fast enough to absorb the stories I heard and the places we saw. When people used to tell me that it was a thrill to actually walk where Jesus walked, I thought they were exaggerating. I could get my fill of the Holy Land through videos, thank you, and spare myself the trip. But they were right. When my foot first touched the soil near the Sea of Galilee, I wept and could not stop weeping. And that was day one.

Our guide, who was a Palestinian Christian, told us many tales we did not know prior to the visit. One of the most disturbing things he shared was that the Romans had a habit of crucifying people, especially Jews, every Friday. These "weekly executions" were meant to intimidate the Jews who were coming into Jerusalem because the people were hung outside the city gates for all passersby to see.

What that meant to me, but was not voiced at the time, was that Jesus had to see those dying people every time he went into town. Imagine what it must have done to his spirit to have to watch people suffer and die, knowing that he had the capability to save them.

Yet he did not. Not at that time, not in that way.

He practiced focused thinking and kept growing in

wisdom and favor until such a time as he was able to effect a far greater change.

It is very easy in this world of distractions and 24/7 information streams to get off track and lose your focus. Knowing what you came here to do, and being determined to do it, no matter what, will give you more power than you can imagine.

Jesus kept his focus.

QUESTIONS

1. What is the Diet Coke can in your life? What is it that you won't allow anyone or anything to disturb?

2. What are some of the distractions, or off-balance maneuvers of other people, that are affecting you?

3. How many distractions can you eliminate?

4. How many distractions do you actually invite?

Dear Lord,
You always kept your focus, no matter what. Please help me to keep my eye on you at all times, for you are my life, my joy, my purpose. Amen.

LEARN TO USE

YOUR SWORD

I HAVE NOT COME TO BRING PEACE, BUT A SWORD.
—MATTHEW 10:34 (NRSV)

I love statues. Nearly every year for Christmas I ship, deliver, or haul in some kind of statue for my friend Catherine's office, kitchen, or garden. After she finally pleaded with me to bring no more 3-D artwork to her, I finally purchased one for myself. It is a life-sized statue of a woman who is wearing a robe. She is barefoot. She has a laurel wreath around her head. In one uplifted hand she is holding a flaming torch. In her other hand she is holding a sword.

I often picture her in my mind when I have a difficult decision to make. She represents wisdom to me—lighting the way to those who seek, yet armed with a sword for cutting away what is false. Wisdom is about both, and that is sometimes a hard lesson to learn.

If I had to choose one of the principles and skills that most helped set me free, it would be that of learning to use the sword. Well-meaning people, and women especially, are prone to needing to be liked by everyone. Indeed, it was Peter's greatest failing, for it was the need for human approval that caused him to deny Christ three times. We seem to learn every word but *no*. The more we desire to serve, the more valuable and desirable we become to others. So, the word *no* needs to be kept handy and dandy at all times—particularly as opportunities begin to multiply exponentially in front of you.

Jesus was a master at cutting away what was false . . . whether it was the hypocrisy of the Pharisees or the illegitimate relationship of the woman at the well. He was adamant that people be unbound and set free. He said, "No!" to the devil three times in the wilderness, and again when Peter tried to get him to change the road to his destiny. His silence when he was on trial cut like a knife into the hearts of those who were falsely accusing him out of their own fears.

I have studied and memorized many poems by the poet Rumi—I love them because they are often so short and to the point. In one of them he writes, "The Hall of Love has ten thousand swords. Don't be afraid to use one." I have quoted that passage many times to people with whom I am working—either in Path Training Seminars or in private consultation. So often it quickly becomes apparent to me that what is holding them back is something that needs to be cut away—a false belief, a distracting "assignment," an unhealthy relationship. Yet as humans, we tend to cling to what is familiar, even if it's pulling us down.

I am certain that if you took the time, became very still and quiet, and asked in prayer, "What do I need to cut away from my life?" the answer would come to you. The question is, Are you willing to make the cut?

Jesus will teach you to use that sword.

QUESTIONS

1. What needs to be cut away in your life?

2. Are you willing to do that?

3. Why or why not?

4. Imagine for five minutes what it might feel like to be free from that bondage.

5. Picture that binding or restricting thing as if it were a wicked plant, trying to wrap itself around your leg and pull you into a swamp. How swiftly and strongly would you react?

6. Why aren't you doing the same thing now?

Dear Lord,
You have given me the sword of your Spirit. Help me use it wisely and well. Amen.

REDEFINE

REALITY

HE WILL GUIDE YOU INTO ALL TRUTH.
—JOHN 16:13

With the plethora of reality shows on television we have taken navel gazing to a fine art. We watch ourselves watching ourselves on television. We set up artificial situations and then call it reality TV. What is reality? According to *Merriam-Webster's Collegiate Dictionary*, reality is "a real event, entity, or state of affairs."

Leadership guru Max DuPree states that the first responsibility of a leader is to define reality. I could sit and chew on that statement for a long, long time. One of the

greatest discoveries of the twentieth century, according to philosopher William James, is the power of human thought to create reality. Look around the room where you are sitting right now, and you will realize that you are surrounded by thoughts that became reality. Someone thought up this computer I am writing on, as well as this sofa I am sitting on, as well as this house I am living in. Everything begins as a sketch somewhere, and that is what makes faith so exciting and so imperative. If I could do one thing to change the world, I think it would be to help people understand the need to become more specific with their faith.

A nonprofit company I started, Path Community Services, was awarded a grant from the Justice Department. The purpose of the grant is to help at-risk youth in El Paso, Texas. Specifically we intend to teach them new ways to conceive their own reality, based on time-honored principles and life skills training. I believe that each person consciously or subconsciously lives out a script that he or she has been given. The question is: Who wrote it?

When Jesus encountered the woman at the well, her script was basically: "fallen woman, living in sin, hiding out from society."

Jesus met her where she was and gave her a new script: "bold woman, excited about life, telling all her friends, supporting new movement."

In *An Essay on Man*, Alexander Pope wrote, "Act well your part, there all the honour lies." Every day in the news

I see people acting out their parts with gusto and fervor—but sometimes their parts need to be changed. Leadership is the art of changing parts or rewriting scripts—of redefining *reality*.

We really do see ourselves as our stories. Which is why we need to look again at the stories we are living and ask if this is the best we can do.

An ancient desert mystic once observed that we are all like nomads, dragging the same tired camels (and excuses) from town to town.

The essence of Christianity is that each person is basically given a new part—a new script—a new reality. Paul wrote about it beautifully: "So for anyone who is in Christ, there is a new creation" (2 Cor. 5:17 NJB).

There is a moment when things can change. A thief on a cross becomes a guest in paradise. A vengeful murderer becomes a loving apostle. A prostitute becomes an example of divine love.

Major changes in script. New realities. All because of Christ and his divine belief in you and me.

When I work with young people, I ask them to do this exercise: pretend that Steven Spielberg has optioned the rights to your life story. He intends to make a full-length feature film about you and has commissioned three writers to submit scripts to him. One script will be about your life as it is now, as if nothing changes. The second script will contain one change of some sort—either you meet a new person or you move to a new place. The third script is the most outrageous of all—you become a totally new person—perhaps the one you always wanted to be—doing the things you always wanted to do. What would that script look like?

If you can fill in the blanks on that one, you have imagination.

If you can see the blanks being filled in, you have faith.

And if you have faith, you have your new reality.

Jesus defined reality.

QUESTIONS

1. Which old stories, like old camels, do you drag with you?

2. What would it be like if you could be handed a new script today? Would you take it?

3. Do you think that you are predestined to mediocrity?

Dear Lord,
You are the Author of reality. Teach me what mine is—in your name. Amen.

BE ASKED

OPEN-ENDED

QUESTIONS

WHO DO YOU SAY THAT I AM?
—MATTHEW 16:15 (NKJV)

My first radio interview was memorable. When the host asked me a question, I smiled and nodded my answer. He had to cover the microphone and remind me that I needed to speak my words out loud in order for the audience to hear me.

I also noticed that he asked open-ended questions, avoiding any questions that could be answered with a simple yes or no. That meant I got a chance to really explain myself and my material. That also meant he had to do less talking.

Just yesterday I received an e-mail that a publisher from another country wanted to purchase the foreign rights to my book, *Teach Your Team to Fish*. The question was, Could they leave out the questions at the end of each chapter because that particular country was not religious by nature? I found it interesting that they were purchasing a book about the team-building qualities of Jesus, yet felt that was not religious. I also found it interesting, and somewhat sad, that they wanted to leave off the questions. (I did grant that permission, grateful that Jesus would be carried into a previously nonreligious venue.)

To me, any and all transformation takes place with the help of the questions. We can sit and read or hear a lecture all day long, but never really take in the material. When we are called upon to answer questions about the material, that means some "registration" has gone on.

Author Peter R. Scholtes states in *The Leader's Handbook*, "In the old organization we asked 'who' questions; 'Who is accountable? Who screwed this up?' In the new organization we ask 'why' or 'how' questions; 'Why has this problem occurred? How can we improve the system and eliminate the cause of this problem?'" He also goes on to say that the new leader as coach seeks collaborative relationships with workers rather than commands and controls. Those who are into directing will have a more challenging time learning to ask good questions—still trying to sneak advice or reprimands into the exchange, saying things such as, "What in the world made you think that was the best way?"

Jesus was famous for his questions. For example, here are a few of the learning questions that Jesus posed:

"Do you want to be healed?"
"Who do you say that I am?"
"Will you wait with me?"
"Philip, how shall we feed these people?"
"Why do you call me Lord, Lord, yet do not do the things I say?"

Open-ended questions convey a host of meanings. For one thing, they convey respect: "I respect your opinion on this matter, and I am waiting for an answer." They also convey connection: "You and I are in this conversation together—it is not a one-sided show. Now it is your turn to create and contribute." They transmit continuation. Because open-ended questions keep the dialogue going, the important ideas being discussed have a chance to grow and breathe—and continue. There is nothing more frustrating than being involved in a one-way conversation where you are having to do all the work conversationally, while the other person simply grunts monosyllabic answers.

One only has to read the Gospels again to realize how much Jesus loved dialoguing and talking about the things of

God. In fact, one of the ideals of a Jewish male in that society was to be able to sit beside the gates and talk about God all day long (while his wife performed the duties spoken of in Proverbs 31). Yet many of our religious traditions have transmitted God from dialogue and discussion to monosyllabic pronouncements, emphasized with thunderclaps or the gavel coming down.

In our rush to seek certainty we shut out wonder.

In our desire to know, we fail to understand what can come only from exploring open-ended questions—getting caught in the tumble and whirl of them, and eventually finding our way out.

Isn't life really an open-ended question?

Whom, then, shall you serve?

Jesus asked open-ended questions.

QUESTIONS

1. Who engages you in dialogue?

2. Who issues pronouncements to you?

3. To which person do you feel more connected?

4. Why do you think Jesus, Son of God, enjoyed open-ended questions so much?

Dear Lord,
I love talking with you, thinking with you, exploring with you. Thank you for having an open mind, full of questions of discovery. Amen.

IDENTIFY YOUR
SOURCE OF LIGHT

IN THY LIGHT SHALL WE SEE LIGHT.
—PSALM 36:9

Growing up with an artist for a mother has given me a keen appreciation for anyone who can render beauty on a blank canvas.

Recently when I took time off to refocus my life and energies, I decided to take an art class at a local university. Even though I had aspirations of discovering a hidden pool of talent that would surprise and delight the masses, I decided to heed my mother's wise advice and take a basic fundamentals of drawing class. Since I'd already learned layout design and composition through my journalism and yearbook editing days, I wanted to skip the first few lessons and just get right into it.

However, I was taken aback when the instructor had us doing a series of drawing exercises without even looking at the page we were drawing on. She explained later that these exercises were designed to help us see the object we were drawing *as it really is*, not how *we think* it looks. She also wanted us to loosen up and get our hands moving across the paper. (There is nothing more terrifying than a blank piece of paper—in art class as in life.)

Another lesson involved sketching simple objects on a table. The instructor said, "Before you begin any drawing you must first identify your source of light. For instance . . . with this vase on the table in front of me . . . where is the light coming from?" We duly noted that it was coming from the window on the left side of the room. "Knowing where the light is coming from will affect every aspect of your drawing. Such items as shading, depth, and volume are affected in major ways by the light source. Learn to identify it before you even begin to sketch. If you leave your drawing and then come back to it later, remember that in order to keep it consistent you must have the same source of light."

I have thought about that lesson many times since then. Probably the fundamental source of any human condition can be traced back to this one question: Where is the source of light?

Jesus was intent on helping people identify their source of light. When he asked the rich young man to go and sell what he had and give the rest to the poor, he was saying, in essence, "Look to your source of light. And don't let it be money."

I have found that anytime I am having a problem, or when I coach people through their own personal obstacle courses, one of the first things that needs to be discerned is where the light is coming from.

Once while I counseled a group of pastors, they noted that their number one problem was exhaustion. I asked them when they were taking their Sabbath rest each week, and they laughed and said, "We don't get a Sabbath rest—we're pastors! We work seven days a week!"

I shared with them the vital need to take a full day of rest and reminded them that even God, the Creator of the universe, didn't work 24/7. They all nodded their heads in agreement. But when I asked them again when their full day of rest was going to be, not one of them would commit to it. Finally they said, "Laurie Beth, we agree with you, but you don't know our congregations. Would you please put in a word to our bosses about our need for rest?"

I did a double take as I struggled to assimilate what I had just heard. I shook my head and said, "Did you hear what you just asked me? My question to you is this: Who is your boss?" Silence reigned in the room. It became clear to me, and perhaps painfully clear to them, that they were not really serving their one Boss, but had many masters. If they were then using public approval as their source of light, no wonder they were leading lives fraught with conflicting agendas and exhaustion.

The very first commandment of the ten we claim to know states, "I am the LORD thy God . . . Thou shalt have no other gods before me" (Ex. 20:2–3). The problems of the early Christians stemmed from this lack of clarity as well—getting clear about who their source of light really was and where it was coming from. Paul exhorted them in the book of Romans not to let works and actions become their source of light, no matter how religious or noble they might be.

When Jesus turned over the tables of the money changers, he was declaring that they were using money as their source of light, not God—even though they were housed just outside the temple. Jesus said, "You cannot serve God and mammon" (Matt. 6:24 NKJV). He was constantly getting his followers to recognize that God, and God alone, was their Source of light.

In the disturbing book and movie *White Oleander* by Jane Fitch, a young girl is thrown into the foster care system after her mother (and only living relative) commits murder. As the social worker drives her out to her new foster home, she says, "You will love your new place. This woman has a heart of gold."

As the girl shyly accepts the introductions, the foster

mom, smacking gum, wearing skintight hip huggers, and smoking a cigarette, asks the girl right out, "Have you accepted Jesus as your personal Savior?" The girl says nothing. Then the woman says, "Well, you will. He has saved me from all my sins, and he can save you from yours, too."

The irony and tragedy of the situation become evident when the foster mom introduces the girl to her boyfriend, Ray, who has wandering eyes and hands. When Ray begins making advances to the girl, the foster mom goes berserk and tells the girl to get out, because "Ray is the best thing that ever happened to me." When the girl persuades her to let her stay, the situation gets worse. In a horrible scene the foster mom pulls a gun and shoots the girl, claiming that she is trying to "steal her man." The gold heart that hangs around the neck of this woman and her words about claiming to know Jesus are empty rhetoric because the real source of "light" in her life is a very flawed man.

As we have watched in horror, CEOs of some of the world's largest companies have been led off to jail in handcuffs. Who and what was their source of light? Priests and bishops, too, have been led off in handcuffs. Who was their source of light? Religious robes and words, fancy offices and big bank accounts do not automatically offer light. Jesus was adamant that only God can be our Light.

I wonder if Jesus was talking to the artist in each of us when he said, "The lamp of the body is the eye. If therefore your eye is good, your whole body will be full of light. But if your eye is bad, your whole body will be full of darkness" (Matt. 6:22–23 NKJV).

Sobering words. The author Kim McMillen wrote in her book, *When I Loved Myself Enough*, "I learned that when I am feeling pain it is because I am living outside the truth."

Jesus said the same thing. Remember where your light is coming from, and then you can begin to see even ashes as a garland in disguise.

QUESTIONS

1. Where is there emotional pain or confusion in your life today?

2. Could it be that you are looking to another source of light for inspiration, and it is falling short?

Dear Lord,
Help me to remember that you are my Source of light in every situation, even when I seem to be sitting in darkness. Amen.

HAVE YOUR

READINESS

ASSESSED

DO YOU WANT TO BE HEALED?
—JOHN 5:6 (CEV)

My friend Catherine's five-year-old granddaughter Briana recently gave me some insight on the importance of readiness. Catherine had spent quite a bit of time helping Briana's older brother, Cal, carve an elaborate pumpkin. Cal and Catherine used several sets of knives and pumpkin paste to come up with the coolest pumpkin Cal could imagine—one that included a face and feet.

When it was time for Briana to carve hers, Catherine explained that because she was younger, she couldn't use all the knives that Cal had used, and that perhaps they should try a pumpkin that had a simple happy face on it rather than one that had feet as well. Briana gave a big "Harrumph!" to that. She reached for the more elaborate knives and said with a voice full of disdain, "Grandma, think about it. I don't want to carve a pumpkin that can't go anywhere!"

Sometimes I think we people, and Christians especially, are like happy-faced pumpkins that have no feet. We have the smile down okay, but we aren't prepared to go anywhere with it.

I am always amazed at how consistently Jesus assessed the readiness of his "clients" before he took them on. "Do you want to be healed?" seems like a throwaway question to a man who had been lying around on a mat for most of his life. Yet Jesus didn't want to just "de-mat" him unless the man himself could admit that he was ready.

People who have turned from therapists into coaches say the major difference between therapy and coaching is that therapy can keep people stirring their stuff for years, never making progress. Yet with coaching, the total emphasis is on "Where do you want to go next?" Good coaches don't want to waste their time, or that of their clients, in moving forward if the heart and mind aren't ready.

Preacher and author Erwin McManus states in his book *An Unstoppable Force* (Group Publishing, 2001) that pastors and leaders don't need to focus on changing what people believe. McManus says, "Basically, we all believe the same thing. What needs to change is what we CARE about. Because only when we care about something, are we willing to take action."

In his book *Sins of the Spirit, Blessings of the Flesh: Lessons for Transforming Evil in Soul and Society,* Matthew Fox claims that we have become a puny and weak-willed society because of the sin of acedia. He defines *acedia* as "a cynical sort of lazy, bored, arrogance." He writes, "Our culture is frankly bored with the word 'sin,' and one reason is that we are bored with everything. We are a species made for cosmology yet our culture has rendered us passive couch potatoes and shopping and entertainment addicts. In short, we have been cut off from the big(ness) of the universe, and consequently we are bored, boring, and violent." Too many of us are living in that lukewarm "saliva" that Jesus talked about so tellingly in the New Testament. We're not ready for change because we are bored and boring.

However, in Tucson there is a church where people meet at 11:00 A.M. on Sundays, then proceed immediately out into the community to feed the homeless, paint over graffiti, or do other good deeds. They call this experience "workship" (www.workship.org).

Jesus as a Coach is ready to go to work. Are you?

QUESTIONS

1. Where in your life are you like the passive pumpkin that has a happy face, but no feet?

2. Where in your life have you become bored and boring?

3. What actions would a casual observer identify as determining your readiness for learning and for life?

Dear Lord,
When you come to me and ask if I want to be healed, I say, "Yes." When you come to me and ask if I want to live, I say, "Yes." I am ready, Lord. Take me, guide me, cut me, show me what it means to be really alive. And most of all, carve me new feet. Amen.

HAVE AN

INDIVIDUALIZED

EDUCATION PLAN

YAHWEH, YOU EXAMINE ME AND KNOW ME,
YOU KNOW WHEN I SIT, WHEN I RISE,
YOU UNDERSTAND MY THOUGHTS FROM AFAR.
—PSALM 139:1–2 (NJB)

In the book *The Heart of Coaching* by Thomas G. Crane, the author lays out an interesting overview of the needs of the various generations and ways to connect with them. The Traditionalist generation, those born between 1925 and 1945, grew up with the Great Depression and World War

Two. Traditionalists value struggle and sacrifice and are familiar and comfortable with delayed gratification. They respect authority, look for job stability and security, and give loyalty to their employers. They and their parents rarely divorced.

The Boomers, those born between 1946 and 1964, grew up in an era of sexual revolution, economic expansion, and consumerism. They divorce frequently, value their feelings, question authority, and place career growth at the top of their lists. Boomers want variety, achievement, and flexibility in their schedules. They often believe that "work is my life."

Xers or Yiffies, born between 1965 and 1980, value learning, involvement, stimulation, and fun. Perhaps as a result of having divorced parents, they are determined to have work not be their lives, but instead give them a life. They are all about networking and technology. In the book *Values Shift* by John P. Izzo and Pamela Withers, we learn that Gen Xers are looking for a place to work that gives them a sense of mission and significance.

We also learn that they value training as a reward, and they prefer to work in teams. This aspect of teaming is also prevalent in the preteen generation. They tend to want brands to help identify who they are, and they look to "persuaders" to tell them everything from how to dress to what to eat and what music to listen to.

I remember working with Pastor Ed Smith and his

incredible team at Zoe Christian Fellowship in Whittier, California. James T. Harris, a friend and Path facilitator, had flown in to work with the church's teenagers while I trained the adults. (Path facilitators are those who have been individually trained to help others discern their mission and vision in life. For more information on this go to my Web site at www.lauriebethjones.com.) It was quite a weekend, with the church grounds flowing with 50 adults and 250 youth all doing activities such as learning their elements, drawing up their talent shields, and writing their one-sentence missions.

One eight-year-old girl, who came forward with two friends alongside to present her talent shield, sticks in my memory. Leticia came forward to the microphone, proudly displaying her talent shield. She said, "I am very good at making people laugh, which is why I drew a happy face. I am great at decorating, which is why I drew a picture of my room. I am good at math, which is why I drew numbers here, and I am a great actress, which is why I have a picture of me winning an Academy Award."

She held up her shield, the audience clapped and cheered, and then she made her way back to her seat. Her two friends dutifully followed her and sat down. I went over and asked the two girls why they went up to the microphone as well. "Oh," they replied, "we just went up to support her."

While my generation grew up valuing the Lone Ranger

and an individualized, Wild West approach to life, the generation of kids born after 1980 is all about team and buddy groups. The young people do not like to think or act alone, and they are even delaying marriage and family building so that they can hang out with their friends.

A wise coach understands that not everyone can be handled the same way. Nor will all people respond to the same incentives.

In one gospel story we are told that Peter complained about an assignment that John had gotten. Jesus reprimanded him, saying, "What is it to you what I ask someone else to do?" He was making it very clear that he wanted to work with one person a certain way, and he had another approach for working with someone else.

The story, found in John 21:20–22 (NJB), reads like this: "Peter turned and saw the disciple whom Jesus loved following them . . . Seeing him, Peter said to Jesus, 'What about him, Lord?' Jesus answered, 'If I want him to stay behind till I come, what does it matter to you? You are to follow me.'" Here Jesus is saying that he has an individual plan and teaching approach for each person he works with. Not all will be called to do the same things or follow the same path.

When it comes to coaching, a cookie-cutter approach doesn't work. Each person is too individual to respond to a one-size-fits-all plan. Anyone who has ever been a parent knows this inherent truth about children. What works with Suzie might not work with Sam, no matter how closely related they are. Yet our educational systems—as well as our business leadership paradigms—often assume that one size fits all.

A number of my friends are in the educational field. They often rail about how children are grouped and taught according to age, when it would better serve them to be grouped and taught according to abilities. Students with special needs are given what is called an IEP, or Individualized Education Plan, which is painstakingly designed and monitored by therapists as well as teachers, school administrators, and others. How wonderful it would be for all students to have an Individualized Education Plan. I believe all adults should have one as well.

One time I sat down with a coaching client of mine after having observed and gotten to know her over a rather intense period. She had attended a Path Training Seminar, which gave me sixteen hours of observation, and we also spent time afterward as she introduced me to a number of her friends, family, and business associates. When our time together was coming to a close, she said, "What do you think I most need?"

I smiled and said, "Would you like me to draw out an IEP for you?" After I explained to her what an Individualized Education Plan was, she eagerly requested it. So, I took a legal pad and said, "My observation is that you are at your highest and best when you have a multiplicity of projects going on. You need to have some under your complete control and authority, and you also need to be part of a larger umbrella organization that gives you a sense of team, protection, and support. You don't need supervision, yet you crave feedback. So, I would allocate your time like this: 30 percent on your own projects, 50 percent on larger team/cause projects, and 20 percent on projects that keep you grounded and require only 'mundane' tasks." I drew this out all quickly for her on the yellow lined paper.

She squealed in delight and grabbed it from me. "This is me! This is exactly what I needed!" she said, and she was on her way.

When Jesus is your Coach, you, too, will be given an Individualized Education Plan. You will be assigned challenges that are uniquely suited to your capabilities and desires.

There is a movie about a training cadet who is constantly being given tests by his supervisor. He enters into sort of a twilight zone when he can't decipher any more what is a test or real danger. The object lesson of the movie is "this is all a test."

I believe that is true about life, too. I believe that we are here on earth to learn how to grow our talents and abilities, which we will put to use in heaven. Those who are faithful with much will be given more. And those who squander what they have will find that they are given even less.

If the gospel says anything to me, it is that Jesus was the Master of a customized, relational approach to God. That makes him a perfect candidate for the coaching job for you and me.

Jesus looked each individual in the eye and said, "I see *you*." The coaching program that he designs for you will not be the same one that he designs for me.

While science may tell us that we have DNA in common with four-legged creatures, I know fraternal twins who are not even remotely alike. Recent studies reveal that clones don't have the same cells after all. Something, somehow, despite our best scientific efforts, inserts itself into the being at the last minute to make it "one of a kind."

Jesus knows every hair on your head . . . and was with you in the womb before you were born. Why not consult with him every day to find out not only why you were made, but also what exactly he had in mind for you to be and do when he created you?

Jesus will give you an Individualized Education Plan.

QUESTIONS

1. What are the challenges you are currently facing?

2. Could it be that they are all individually and specifically designed for your growth?

3. Which part of the growth don't you want?

4. If you turn away from your current challenges, where do you expect your growth to come from?

Dear Lord,

You have designed an individualized set of challenges for me, specifically designed to help me grow into the fullness you have for me. Help me not turn away from what is before me, but move toward it with faith, trust, and fearlessness. Amen.

BE SEEN

HE ENTERED JERICHO AND WAS GOING THROUGH
THE TOWN AND SUDDENLY A MAN WHOSE NAME WAS
ZACCHAEUS MADE HIS APPEARANCE; HE WAS ONE OF
THE SENIOR TAX COLLECTORS AND A WEALTHY MAN. HE
KEPT TRYING TO SEE WHICH JESUS WAS, BUT HE WAS
TOO SHORT AND COULD NOT SEE HIM FOR THE CROWD;
SO HE RAN AHEAD AND CLIMBED A SYCAMORE TREE TO
CATCH A GLIMPSE OF JESUS WHO WAS TO PASS THAT
WAY. WHEN JESUS REACHED THE SPOT HE LOOKED UP
AND SPOKE TO HIM, "ZACCHAEUS, COME DOWN."
—LUKE 19:1–5 (NJB)

Perhaps many of us can relate to Zacchaeus, the man who preferred watching things from afar. Maybe he was in the tree because he was little and couldn't see above the crowd. Or maybe he was enjoying putting a little distance between himself and what was going on with this Jesus fellow. Imagine his surprise when Jesus stopped walking, looked up in the tree, and said, "Zacchaeus, I see you. Come on down from there and let's start interacting one on one."

I have a unique, one-on-one relationship with Jesus. My relationship with Jesus does not and cannot look like your relationship with Jesus, or it wouldn't be unique.

When I first began to fall in love with Jesus, I was a teenager. I decided that we would have nicknames for each other, and we do. I also requested that we have a little personal ritual that is ours, and I will share it with you. It is this: I have asked that whenever he is thinking about me, he is to send me a ladybug. It was a simple request made years ago. But since that time I have been amazed and delighted at how inventive and romantic and thoughtful my Lover can be.

These incidents are true.

Once I was in Toledo, Ohio, driving in a snowstorm. I was very tired and discouraged and not too happy about my consulting assignment there, even though I loved the people. I got out of my rented car, turned to lock the door, and found a ladybug on my windshield—in the snow! True story.

Next true story. I was in a lonely hotel room in a little town way outside Dallas, Texas, preparing to speak to a group of prison chaplains. I was tired. It had been a long flight. I was questioning why I had agreed to this particular assignment. I was hungry. The restaurants were closed. There was no room service. I sighed and sat down to open my computer in order to check my e-mails. As I raised the screen on my laptop, a ladybug landed on it. Understand this was in a hotel room, with closed windows, in a desert town, during winter. God was saying, "I see you. I love you. I'm with you."

Another true story. I was in the Bahamas, luxuriating in *this* particular assignment. I had about two hours before my presentation, and I decided to take a very early morning swim. I stole out to the pool around five o'clock in the morning, slipped into the water, and began doing my laps. There, in the middle of the pool, floating right in front of me, was a ladybug. God was saying, "I see you. I'm with you. I love you."

You can do this, too. One friend has an agreement with God about white butterflies. (Joan of Arc was said to have this agreement, too, and to have often been seen marching off to war, surrounded by white butterflies.) Another friend has an understanding with God about finding pennies where she least expects them. She tells the story of how every day, no matter where she is, she will always find a penny and know that God is thinking about her. One day she was diagnosed with breast cancer. As she lay in the hospital room, facing her surgery, she realized that for the first time in twenty-six years, she had gone all day without finding a penny from heaven. Then an orderly walked in and said, "I was just about to go off my shift, and I found this penny right outside your room. For some reason, I needed to bring it to you." God was saying to her, "I see you. I love you. I'm here."

My sister, Kathy, experienced an amazing display of God's customized and gentle communication. Kathy and our grandmother, Mamgu (pronounced "maam gee,"which is Welsh for grandmother), had a very close and loving relationship. As Mamgu got older, she said, "Kathy, I want to give you something that will always comfort you, as it has me throughout the years." She reached up in the closet and brought down a beautiful cobalt blue teapot with gold filigree trim around the edges. She said, "My grandmother gave this to me, and I want to give it to you. Whenever you lift up this lid, I want you to feel my presence with you." Mamgu died shortly afterward, and Kathy kept the teapot as a very special treasure.

One night an electrical storm hit the farmhouse where Kathy and her family lived. A power surge went from the outlet to my niece Tara's metal bed and then leaped onto the curtains. Within minutes Tara's room was in flames.

She ran and alerted everyone that the house was on fire, and they all made their way out into the fields. Since they lived so far out of town, and there was no water pressure to speak of, they all stood barefoot in the midnight chill and watched their house burn to the ground.

My sister was devastated. Unless you have experienced your home burning to the ground, taking all your memories with it, you can't imagine how emotionally draining it is. Kathy went back with the family the next day and began sifting through the ashes. There, in the middle of what had been the living room, was the little blue teapot. It was unharmed, even though all around it lay melted glassware and broken dishes that had fallen from the shelves. It stood alone, blue and bright, in the midst of ashes. She lifted up the lid and heard, "I am with you." And she wept. God and her grandmother were saying, "I see you. I'm with you. I love you."

Jesus is saying, "I see you."

QUESTIONS

1. Do you have a little love ritual with God?

2. If not, why not?

3. If so, what is it?

4. Do you believe that God sees you right where you are?

5. Do you believe that you are worthy of a special ritual? (You are.)

Dear Lord,

Thank you for ladybugs and bright shiny pennies and little blue teapots, and for the love you shine so generously on all of us every day. I love you. Amen.

HAVE
FUN

MY SOUL SHALL BE JOYFUL IN MY GOD.
—ISAIAH 61:10

I had the privilege of shadowing a leading speech pathologist in Phoenix as she went about the town on her daily
rounds, meeting with groups of children who had been
identified as having speech disabilities. As I helped her
unload her trunk to carry in her working tools, I was mysti-
fied that one of the boxes was filled with coloring books,
crayons, playing cards, and candy. While she dutifully carried in her computer and miniprinter, I volunteered to assist
her with the box of toys.

The minute the children saw her, they jumped up from their desks and ran into the speech room, wiggling eagerly into their chairs and looking at her with smiling faces. She introduced me as Ms. Jones, a friend who was there to help, and my heart began to melt as I saw the precious and precocious imprints of who they were and who they were to be.

One little boy named Jonathan looked at me quizzically and said, "Are you from Texath?"

"Yes," I said and smiled, "I am. How did you know?"

He grinned back at me and said, "I juth guethed."

A little girl with a pigtail and a missing tooth showed me her drawing.

"What is that a picture of?" I asked her.

She said, "It's a picture of my two puppies."

"What is the name of the picture?" I asked.

She looked at it a moment and then giggled. "I call it 'Lots of Lup.'"

Then Shelly proceeded to get out a deck of picture cards, deal them in sixes to the kids, and lead them in a game of Fish. She took out her drill sheets and began noting with x's and o's the sounds they were or were not executing successfully. She did this while they played, however.

"Jonathan, do you have a turtle?" asked Lisa.

"No—go fith!" Jonathan declared.

When Shelly noticed a letter that was being mispronounced, she gently corrected him and then had him go through a quick series of drills. She told him to say, "See, sigh, so, say, keeping your teeth together," which Jonathan did, smiling all the while.

Shelly did this with each child, making quick notes while still keeping eye contact with him or her. As the kids giggled and squirmed, she let them have conversations, one of which included a Kent-to-Billy exchange that went: "Billy, you're not supposed to lick the cards!"

At the end of the game Shelly gave two colored Gummy Bears to each participant, and stickers to the two children who had most improved. The hour flew by, and kids left asking when she was coming back again.

In another class she had them do drawings and then tell a story about what was going on in the drawing, praising not only their artwork but also their correct use of new letters.

Shelly has one of the fastest-growing practices in Phoenix, and the State Department recommends her as a professional who gets results. At the same time she has kids eagerly awaiting her classes. Shelly succeeds, in part, because she makes the learning fun—keeps it quick and interesting, and hands out little, incremental, tangible, and delightful rewards.

As I was sharing this story with a fellow speaker, he said, "I wish she had been the one to work with my daughter. She stuttered for years in grade school. The man they sent to work with her was like a drill sergeant—very tough, demanding, and stern. My daughter dreaded going to class with him. Eventually she just clammed up around him altogether. She stutters to this day."

Good coaches keep things moving, interesting, and fun, and Jesus modeled that consistently in his behavior with his team. No two days or conversations were ever alike, whether they were having a picnic on the shore or casting demons into pigs by the sea.

Jesus kept the flow of conversation relevant and timely, inserting key questions at specific points that made the disciples stop, think, and apply.

As he and Philip and the rest of the team watched with growing amazement the numbers of people multiply on the shore, Jesus turned to him and asked, "Philip, how are we going to feed these people?" It was a major and timely learning opportunity for Philip, who then had to consider how to answer the question.

Jesus, Coach, was a master at asking the ticklish question . . . the one that seemed to have no apparent answer. He kept their minds in motion and made it fun. That was one reason the apostles followed him (and one reason others will follow you).

QUESTIONS

1. Do your associates eagerly await the next visit with you, or dread it?

2. What question might Jesus, Coach, ask you about the situation you are currently facing?

3. What are you doing to encourage Jesus as a Coach to want to hang around you?

Dear Lord,
As Creator of the universe, you have a mind that never stops thinking and growing. Help me be more open to having fun with you and engaging you quickly and constantly on a daily basis. Amen.

Overcome

Procrastination

BLESSED ARE THOSE WHO HEAR
THE WORD . . . AND KEEP IT!
—LUKE 11:28 (NKJV)

Today as I was loading five bags of garbage into my rental car, it occurred to me that procrastination is the biggest energy leak a person can have. I was thinking this because I meant to take out the garbage last night so it would be there for the early-morning pickup. But when I came in the door after a long day, I thought, *Oh, I'll get it later.* Of course later meant it didn't happen. So I missed this week's garbage run and will have to load the garbage into my car and take it to a city dump.

Since I am house sitting for a friend in a city I am unfamiliar with, I now have to make numerous phone calls to determine where the city dump is. What a lovely way to spend my morning. I could have prevented this by spending a more focused five minutes last night. Time is the most expensive nonrenewable commodity we have on this earth, and I just wasted hours of it.

Last week I heard a sermon, based on Matthew 25, about the late virgins—specifically the five virgins who couldn't be bothered to get oil for their lamps for the wedding, which was imminent.

When the Bridegroom didn't show up on time, the five other virgins who had gone to the trouble to get extra oil for their lamps had enough to last the night. The procrastinating virgins ("Oh, we'll get it later") missed the entire wedding party. In other words, their procrastination kept them out of the kingdom of heaven. Rough penalty for a little "tomorrow" thinking.

When Jesus said to Peter, "Drop your nets and follow me," he didn't say, "Mañana." He meant, *"Now!"* When Elisha met Elijah, he immediately took action—slaying his oxen and burning his plow on the spot in order to follow his new calling. Elisha became one of the most powerful prophets in history. When Joseph was told in a dream to take Mary and baby Jesus to Egypt to escape the wrath of King Herod, he didn't wait until he had vacation time. He bundled them up immediately and headed out the door.

Jesus was action oriented. In fact, he was so action oriented that he had to be nailed to the cross to keep him from doing more.

Even from the cross he was delegating: "Mary, this is your new son, John. John, this is your new mother." With his dying breath Jesus was using his talents and his influence to make the world a better place.

One hallmark of highly effective people is that they have a sense of urgency about the importance of even the smallest task. Yet all too many of us operate in sort of a mind fog that seems to tell us to "slow down, take it easy, don't sweat the small stuff." Small stuff not acted upon becomes big stuff that consumes you. (This is not to confuse worry with action. In fact, one of the greatest antidotes to worry *is* taking action—*now*.)

Time-efficiency experts tell us to handle a sheet of paper only one time. Act on it, file it, or throw it away. Don't let it just lie there, accumulating dust. Too many of us do that with our thoughts and ideas, however. We let them just sit there, accumulating dust, and then complain when someone else acts on them.

At a recent International Conference on Coaching Summit, a group of executive coaches were pondering what five provocative questions they could ask their clients that would cause them to move further faster. Nobody seemed to have the real top five. I've been thinking about it for some time. I am now convinced that one of the top five questions ought to be this: "What are you avoiding doing that you know needs to be done?" Imagine the discussions that could flow out of that one. We seem to have a talent for burying the truth, covering it up, distracting ourselves from it.

This only keeps us in the sluggish zone—financially, emotionally, and spiritually. Jesus said that "you will know the truth, and the truth will set you free" (John 8:32 NLT); he was teaching that delaying and distracting habits hinder us.

He said as much to the woman at the well in John 4:5–28. When she tried to launch into a discourse about some esoteric theology, he said, "Go and get your husband." She did not want to admit that she was living with a man outside of marriage, yet Jesus wanted her to get straight to that issue—not so that he could condemn her, but so that she could face it and then get free.

Yesterday I was observing a water aerobics course at a deluxe health spa in Phoenix. Not being able to enter the pool for my lap swim due to a prescheduled class that was taking place there, I decided to watch and wait. One woman arrived late to the group of six who apparently knew each other well. This woman was wearing a bright pink bathing suit and had all the matching accessories.

She reminded me of one of the dancing elephants in the movie *Fantasia* because she was extremely large, yet seemed to balance everything very delicately. Before she got in the water, she produced an elaborate chlorine testing kit and proceeded to dip it in several times while the other women and the instructor were exercising away. She took the chlorine reading three times, and only after the third time did she proceed into the water. Since she was already thirty minutes late, she missed half the class. Add another five minutes for the fancy lab test, and that made it thirty-five minutes late.

When the class ended, I heard her explaining in a rather superior tone to the other women that chlorine at high levels can cause your skin to itch, and she didn't want to have itchy skin. I couldn't help noticing how her priorities were causing her to miss the benefits of the class. The most apparent health issue she was facing was being extremely overweight. Yet most of her attention was on the condition of her skin. Dipping a paper strip into the water is much easier than lunging your body through it at a high and consistent musical pace. I chuckled at this woman's behavior because we are all so much like her, are we not?

We often choose the complicated route—the route that also causes us somehow to have special attention—when if we just went straight at the challenges facing us, we'd have the problem beaten in no time. It is the old "elephant in the living room" syndrome. People are complaining about the dirty dishes in the sink when the elephant of huge, unresolved issues is trashing their home.

Procrastination seems like a harmless and benign habit. We even make jokes about it—perhaps because it is a characteristic that lives with us all. But the truth is, procrastination is costly. And Jesus said it can cost you everything.

When the virgins asked the Bridegroom to be permitted into the party, he said harshly, "I do not know you." He didn't say, "Okay, gals, come on in. I was only joking."

There is a time when the time is too late. Decisions delayed can cause major damage (or heartache). Lives have been ruined because of this habit.

A woman I knew was always complaining about how chaotic and out of control her life was. She asked me to coach her through some major transitions. I did for a while until I quit in frustration. I observed that every major problem in her life was not caused by the villains she initially pointed to—her ex-husband, her boss, her daughter, and her banker—but by the fact she never made a decision! She hemmed and hawed about this or that until ultimately someone was forced to decide for her, and then she complained endlessly about how bad that decision was. Not to decide *is* to decide.

Passive-aggressive people use procrastination as an ally. By not taking action, they force others to take action for them, and then they complain about not being involved in the decision making.

Leaders know that nearly half of all the decisions they

make might be wrong. They can weigh all the evidence and still not have enough to go on. Ultimately they play the odds and take action.

There is a difference between waiting on the Lord through obedience and just plain waiting. Or delaying. Or deciding to wait until the sky clears up or the fear goes away. If you are moving forward toward your vision, the fear will never go away.

Don't let procrastination destroy you—in big or little ways. Author Robert Kiyosaki in his book, *Rich Dad, Poor Dad* (Warner Books, 2000), says that "excuses are the loser in you talking." Procrastination feeds on excuses and spits them out regularly.

Jesus will always encourage you to take action toward the good. And that means *now!*

QUESTIONS

1. What action that you know you need to take are you currently avoiding?

2. Why?

3. If procrastination is the loser in you talking, what would the winner in you say?

Dear Lord,

Your wonders never cease. Your patience is unending. Yet there is a time for everything good that needs to be done, and that time is always now. Help me eliminate procrastination in my life so that I can see you, right now, more clearly, rather than have you floating hazily in the fog of my tomorrows. Amen.

USE YOUR

GREATEST

STRENGTH

YOU WILL USE A TALENT OF PURE GOLD FOR THE
LAMP-STAND AND ALL ITS ACCESSORIES; AND SEE
THAT YOU WORK TO THE DESIGN WHICH WAS
SHOWN YOU ON THE MOUNTAIN.
—EXODUS 25:39–40 (NJB)

God was very specific about the materials and design that
were to be used in the construction of the temple.
Craftsmanship and quality were paramount in building his
house, and the work was to be done according to the design
shown to Moses on the mountain.

I like to think of this passage as it applies to building teams, companies, and organizations as well. We are to engage the finest craftspeople, allowing them to use their most pure "talents," and have them follow a design given to them from on high. Does this really happen?

The Gallup organization recently surveyed more than two million workers in 101 companies around the world. One question was this: "Do you get to use your greatest strength every day at work?"

Eighty percent, *or eight out of ten people* said that they do not get to use their greatest strength every day at work. Imagine what we could do organizationally and teamwise if people's highest gifts were identified and unleashed. Essentially we are operating at only 20 percent capacity. *What a waste of time, energy, and talent!*

Jesus went from being a carpenter to being a preacher. I often imagine what went through his mind the day he finally lay the hammer down and walked out the door, closing the shop for the very last time.

When I had the privilege of being in Jerusalem in 1999, our guide, a Palestinian Christian, shared with us that the term that was used for Jesus was *tekton*, which means not only "carpenter," but also "craftsman." Jesus was obviously very skilled at what he did with his hands. I'm sure he could take a block of wood and shape it into an oxen yoke that was so customized it caused no blisters. That was essential for the people of his village, because if their ox could not plow the field, due to an injury or blister, then the family did not eat. He was conscientious about his work.

Yet there burned in him a driving force that went beyond his trained skill level. His highest gift ultimately led him from the safety of a carpenter's workbench into the desert wilderness, where he had to confront his greatest fears and move on.

Every temptation that Jesus faced in the wilderness was related to his higher gifts.

Could he have turned those stones into bread when he was so hungry? Yes. But he didn't. In every case where he was called to use his higher gifts for a lesser purpose, Jesus refused. That restraint allowed him to use his gifts in their highest form.

Jesus determined that he would not use his higher gifts for selfish purposes. Yet he also determined that he would indeed use them.

In the book *Recognizing Your Strengths* by Marcus Buckingham and Donald O. Clifton, Ph.D., the authors confront some very basic, if errant, paradigms present in this country. One paradigm is that you must work to overcome your weaknesses in order to be more effective. They say, "Forget about your weaknesses—get keyed in on your strengths. That is how you grow." We still hold dear the myths of the well-rounded employee and the perfect spouse. We not only read these myths to our children, but we also believe them. "Someday our prince will come" is translated into "Someday I will find the perfect spouse . . . or company . . . or job."

The essential thing is to realize what your strengths are and then refine them. This principle has been among the most life-changing and beneficial ones I've ever adopted. Once I realized that I was cut out to be a speaker and an author, rather than a social worker or administrator, my work took off. I remember that I took several accounting courses in college, knowing that someday I wanted to run my own business. (My mother was a bookkeeper for thirty-seven years.) I remember taking the courses, but to this day I cannot tell you much, if anything, about accounting. My basic system is boiled down to three words. There is either *enough* or *not enough*. Simple, eh? To this day Oprah Winfrey, a newly minted billionaire, cannot read a balance or a profit and loss sheet. Imagine what we would have lost if she had gone into the accounting business—because that was her weakest link.

In the book *Recognizing Your Strengths*, I highlighted and underlined and bent the page corner on this statement: "Perhaps the highest use of our schools would be to help children identify their greatest strengths."

Jesus doesn't teach about weakest links. He teaches about finding our highest callings and strengths, and going after them with all our hearts.

Jesus used his greatest strength.

QUESTIONS

1. How could it be that skills and strengths might not be the same?

2. Do you know your greatest strength? What is it?

3. What would it be like to be able to use your greatest strength every day?

Dear Lord,
Help me see where my light is truly lit by you, and then set it on a lamp stand, not under a bushel. Amen.

BE OFF TO A
ROUGH START

WHAT DO YOU WANT FROM ME?
MY HOUR HAS NOT COME YET.
—JOHN 2:4 (NJB)

In coaching sessions I've observed that many clients want to do things perfectly right out of the gate. You and I might have emerged perfectly from the womb at birth, but even if we did have all body parts intact, the whole process for most of us was a bloody, painful, and at times a screaming mess.

The problem with our culture, which worships success and achievement, is that those states are not really states at all, but more like parts of a bumpy, ugly, and very uncertain process.

Jerry Seinfeld has become perhaps the highest paid and most famous male stand-up comedian of our time. He has the capability to make us laugh about nothing . . . and was able to take the concept of little things and get us to laugh with him for seven years. Near the end of his television show, which he left voluntarily, he was being paid $1 million per episode. That is how much we liked him and how good he was at what he did.

Yet the first time he did stand-up comedy, he wasn't so good. He had been preparing for it for a long time—ever since he was a kid. He listened nonstop to albums by Bill Cosby. He used to follow his father around and write down jokes, loving more than anything to make his classmates laugh.

He did the dutiful thing his parents requested and got his college degree. Yet the very night he graduated from college, he didn't go to a party. He went to a local comedy club in New York—sort of a karaoke-type place—and mustered up his courage and walked on stage. When the spotlight hit him, all the jokes he had prepared escaped him. He said that he could remember only the general topics. So he stood there in his suit and said single words: "Delis. Cousins. Roommates. Girlfriends." He could not remember a single sentence that went with each topic! Yet to his amazement, the people laughed. They liked him. He got off stage in a minute and a half and resolved next time that he would rehearse and memorize every single sentence—not just the topics. The next week, when he went back, he got even more laughs, and he was hooked.

Yet his career didn't zoom off from there. He hung around comedy clubs enough to get a job as an emcee. Then he got his own HBO special. Then he was offered a part on another comedy show. Then he got fired. They said he couldn't act.

Then he was offered yet another show. That time they handed him more scripted lines. Again he was fired.

By then, he said he was going to do a show and write his own lines. He got a show. It was criticized as being a show about nothing. Instead of being discouraged by that comment, he took it to heart and decided to *make that his theme!*

His show was liked, but it wasn't that well liked. It was shelved for a time. Then network execs resurrected it. Then they moved it around.

Yet Jerry never lost sight of his focus and his greatest strength, which was to make people laugh. He said he didn't care if he did that on a television show or on the road. Finally his audience found him, and he found his audience. Jerry Seinfeld's "show about nothing" became one of the most successful comedy shows of all time.

I love stories like that. When I encountered Jerry's show, it was already very well watched. I was a latecomer fan, and so his success was all I knew. Only by reading about his background did I learn about his false start, his getting fired, his show being shelved, and all the other bumps in the road. What if Jerry had decided that because he forgot his lines the first night of stand-up, he wasn't "meant to be" a comedian? What if the first hecklers he encountered had driven him off the stage? What if he had let the critics' arrows pierce his heart instead of turn into a rocket that carried him to stardom?

Jerry was willing to begin with a rough start, and only later did the way become smooth.

When Jesus did his first miracle, by all accounts it wasn't really his idea. His mother asked him to help solve a problem at a party:

On the third day a wedding took place at Cana in Galilee. Jesus' mother was there, and Jesus and his disciples had also been invited to the wedding. When the wine was gone, Jesus' mother said to him, "They have no more wine."

"Dear woman, why do you involve me?" Jesus replied, "My time has not yet come."

His mother said to the servants, "Do whatever he tells you." Nearby stood six stone water jars, the kind used by the Jews for ceremonial washing, each holding from twenty to thirty gallons. Jesus said to the servants, "Fill the jars with water"; so they filled them to the brim. Then he told them, "Now draw some out and take it to the master of the banquet." They did so, and the master of the banquet tasted the water that had been turned into wine. He did not realize where it had come from, though the servants who had drawn the water knew. Then he called the bridegroom aside and said, "Everyone brings out the choice wine first and then the cheaper wine after the guests have had too much to drink; but you have saved the best till now." (John 2:1–10 NIV)

We learn from the gospel account how rough a beginning it was. Yet Jesus did what he was asked to do, even if it wasn't the ideal time and place, according to his original plan.

Perhaps friends or family members are pressuring you to do something that they know you are very good at, yet you are resisting, telling them it's not the right time or place or reason. Maybe, you think that there might be a more appropriate, glorious, or otherwise different way or place to make your talents known.

Yet I am thinking right now of many biblical heroes and heroines who were pressed into service not of their own accord, but at someone else's request.

Perhaps you remember the story of Mordecai and Esther, recounted so compellingly in the book of Esther. Esther was unwillingly pressed into service as a harem girl and later became queen. She was warned by her cousin Moredecai not to reveal that she was a Jew, which no doubt put added pressure on her less-than-ideal circumstances. Yet her beauty and grace of manner caused her to be the king's favorite.

When the king became drunk and allowed a misguided associate to persuade him to eliminate all the Jews, Mordecai went to Esther (who had become queen by that time) and pleaded with her to reveal that she was a Jew and ask for the king's retraction of his edict. Esther, understandably, was afraid.

Yet Mordecai told her, "Do not suppose that, because you are in the king's palace, you are going to be the one Jew to escape. No; if you persist in remaining silent at such a time, relief and deliverance will come to the Jews from another quarter, but both you and your father's whole family will perish. Who knows? Perhaps you have to come to the throne for just such a time as this" (Est. 4:12–14 NJB). Mordecai impressed upon Esther that maybe it was the time for her to use her influence and grace.

Her reluctance and fear gave way to courage. She decided to fast and pray, and uncertain of success, she said, "If I perish, I perish" (Est. 4:16 NJB). Her path had no red carpet—only tentative steps, taken in fear, after being pushed from behind.

Esther was willing to have a rough start. Are you?

QUESTIONS

1. Do you tend to want to do things "right" the first time?

2. Could it be that you are really just procrastinating and using other "obstacles" as an excuse not to act?

3. Can you name others who got off to a rough start? (Abraham Lincoln, for example, lost his first two elections for public office, but won the third.)

Dear Lord,
You are willing to work from chaos and formlessness to do your best work. Help me do the same. Amen.

BALANCE

My dear friend Robin Wood shared with me a story that I want to pass on to you. She said that she was invited to go ice-skating with her son, his friends, and their moms at the local ice-skating rink in Cincinnati. Robin said the three moms hit it off instantly and began to hang out in the "Moms" section of the ice. Inspired by the recent winter Olympics, all three of them were attempting to do spiral spins and swirls.

Yet Robin said that she took one spin on the ice and immediately collapsed upon herself, grateful that her son was too far off to see her ending up as a coated clump of gray on the ice. Another mother, Cecilia, did a little better but quickly lost her balance in the swirling and also tumbled into a heap.

Jennifer, however, easily negotiated a perfect swirl and spin, even though she had never been on the ice before.

When the other two mothers looked up at her in awe and asked how she did it, she replied, "I was trained as a ballerina. I learned how to keep my balance." When they asked her the secret to keeping her balance, she replied, "I was taught how to find my 'center,' and whenever I begin to feel off center, I instantly return to it."

How simple. How profound. Yet until we know where our "center" is, we will be wobbly, off-balance, and probably at odds with the world and ourselves. Once we hit that "sweet spot," we can remember to return to it again and again.

Keeping your balance means being able to swiftly and surely deal with temptations, as Jesus did. Keeping your balance means not being swayed by the cheers of the roaring crowd, wanting you to be something you are not. Being centered means being able to turn the other cheek and answer not a word, just as Jesus did. Being centered means that you can die at any time and still know that you died doing God's will, just as Jesus did.

The world is trying to find its center—through artificial highs or artificial means. Being centered—oh, the power of that. You know it when you see it. You'll know it when you have it.

And once you attain the balance of being "centered," you will always know how to find it again, just as Jesus did.

This section is about balance—the one thing that people often are lacking, even when they seem to have it all.

HAVE HELP
TO FIND
YOUR BALANCE

SEEK FIRST THE KINGDOM OF GOD . . . AND ALL
THESE THINGS SHALL BE ADDED TO YOU.
—MATTHEW 6:33 (NKJV)

Watching the news will drive anyone to distraction, partly because of the constantly crawling news bites that are positioned right under the constantly talking newscasters. It would seem that our cultural belief is that if we just get *enough information fast enough*, we'll get it right. Unfortunately one only has to hear the news to understand that we are not getting it right, but are getting it wrong constantly. What is needed perhaps more than information is wisdom, and wisdom comes from balance.

When I met recently with leaders of one of the largest companies in the world, they were saying, "We are telling our people with one side of our mouths, 'Take time for your family.' And with the other side of our mouths we are saying, 'Give us all you've got.' And the truth is, we *are* talking out of both sides of our mouths, and that is the reality of this day and age."

Who among us doesn't have competing demands? Being spiritual doesn't necessarily ensure that you will have balance either; pastors are among the most exhausted and harried servants among us. Being rich doesn't ensure balance; the wealthy sometimes "greed" themselves into bankruptcy or jail.

According to one Harvard researcher, people today are seeking products or companies that will help them find a balance in their lives. And it isn't easy.

Much has been written about Baby Boomers who were raised to believe that we could have it all. Women Baby Boomers were profiled in the *Harvard Business Review*, in an article by Sylvia Ann Hewlett, titled "Executive Women and the Myth of Having It All." She draws her conclusions from research she conducted for her book *Creating a Life: Professional Women and the Quest for Children*. In this article Hewlett states that "at midlife, between a third and a half of all successful career women in the United States do not have children." It is not necessarily that they do not want to have children, but that for many women, the demands of ambitious careers, the asymmetries of male-female relationships, and the difficulties of bearing children late in life crowd out the possibilities of having children. Hewlett writes that the goal of her work is "to generate workplace policies that recognize the huge costs to business of losing highly educated women when they start their families." She also hopes "to galvanize young women to make newly urgent demands of their partners, employers, and policy makers and thus create more generous life choices for themselves." Basically her advice to young women seeking to "have it all" is this:

1. Figure out what you want your life to look like at forty-five.

2. If you want to have a family, give urgent priority to finding a partner in your twenties and thirties.

3. Have your first child before the age of thirty-five.

4. Choose a career that will give you the gift of time.

5. Choose a company that will help you achieve work-life balance.

Her advice to corporate America is this:

1. Create a time bank for paid parenting leave, allowing three months of paid leave, which could be taken as needed until the child turns eighteen.

2. Restructure retirement plans to eliminate penalties for career interruptions.

3. Allow career breaks of up to three years, which are unpaid, but allow for assurances of a job upon return.

4. Create high-level jobs that have reduced-hour workloads that still offer possibilities of promotion.

5. Allow alumni status for former employees.

A number of corporations are stepping up to the plate and are profiled in magazines such as *Fortune* and *Working Woman*. However, more needs to be done.

While waiting in a doctor's office the other day I read with interest in *People* magazine the story of Mary Matalin, advisor to Vice President Dick Cheney, and her choice to return home. The seventy-hour workweeks, constant travel, and stresses regarding security were taking their toll on Mary, her husband, James, and their two little girls. Yet it was one day when James called, crying, that turned Mary around.

Their daughter Mattie had gone to school to participate in career day. While other students showed up with complex schematics constructed with meticulous parental help, Mattie showed up carrying only a blackboard, a piece of chalk, and an apple to convey her career choice as teacher. Neither James, himself a highly paid political consultant, nor Mary had taken the time to assist Mattie in her project, and James was in tears. Both of them decided that it wasn't right, and Mary told the vice president good-bye.

Another phenomenon that we are encountering is the role reversals of women at work. One friend of mine told me this story about her daughter, "Julie." Julie jets around the world, makes decisions affecting hundreds of people a day, and is used to selecting her own wine. When I went to dinner with Julie and her fiancé, I was amused that Julie selected the table, ordered the wine, approved the wine, and made all the menu decisions. What followed was a true discussion.

Mark, the young fiancé, asked, "Julie, are you going to be in town for Valentine's Day?"

Julie replied that she was not, but that she would arrive the following morning.

Mark began to pout, saying in a whining tone, "You are going to miss our first Valentine's Day together?"

Julie replied, somewhat irritated, "Valentine's Day is just another day on a calendar. I'll make it up to you the following day, okay?"

Realizing the humor in the situation, Mark said good-naturedly, "Look, Julie, one of us has to be the whiny wife in this relationship, and it looks like it is going to be me."

Roles are up for grabs these days, as are many of the once tried-and-true rules. How shall we find our way?

Jesus taught us how to find our balance, and his words apply to us today: "Seek first the kingdom of God . . . and all these things shall be added to you."

How simple balance is—if we know where we stand and what we are looking for.

QUESTIONS

1. Why is it so easy to lose our balance these days?

2. Why isn't "information" the answer to the balance question?

3. How can seeking first the kingdom of God help you find your balance?

4. Why is it so difficult for people, especially women, to "have it all"?

Dear Lord,
Help me understand that you are my center of gravity. Help me choose wisely when other lives are affected. Help me discern ambition from calling, and heart's desires from consumer's call. Amen.

KNOW THAT
YOUR LADDER
IS SECURE

I WILL NEVER LEAVE YOU NOR FORSAKE YOU.
—HEBREWS 13:5 (NKJV)

Recently a friend and I went to the New Mexico state fair. As we were walking around the fairgrounds on a beautiful fall evening, we began to challenge each other to attempt some of the games and contests heralded by neon lights and dangling stuffed animals too large to carry home. She attempted, and lost, the ring-throwing contest. I attempted, and lost, the sharp-shooter contest. Then we came upon "The Pirate's Ladder."

Set at an angle and stretched over airbags, the ladder was relatively short. The contest looked simple. Merely climb the twelve-foot stretch and ring the red buzzer to win. The attendant promoting the contest ambled up the ladder easily—sometimes doing it on all fours and sometimes doing it standing straight up. How hard could it be?

My friend got up on the ladder and immediately flipped over. He asked her to try again. This time she got up three of the ten rungs and again flipped over.

He asked if she wanted him to hold the ladder for her, and on her behalf I interceded, "Yes!" So, he leaned down and held the ladder steady for her, and she was able to make it up.

As she laughingly conceded that the task was too difficult for her without his help, she asked how he did it. He smiled and lifted up his shirt to reveal a set of highly developed six-pack abs. "Balance isn't in your head. It's in your guts," he said and then turned to the next customer.

I thought about that a lot as we walked back to the car. There seemed to be a twofold lesson in that encounter. One was that as long as he was holding the ladder, she was able to get a lot farther. She never looked back to make sure he wasn't going to let her fall she trusted that he would do what he said he would do. The second lesson was that balance isn't in your head—it's in your guts. No amount of mental calculation would allow her to get up that ladder—unless she also had the guts to try.

At a party in New York I had a chance to visit with a woman who coordinates top-level meetings with some of the world's "centillionaires." She said it seems that one prerequisite of these meetings is having your own Lear jet. The meeting, held at resort locations around the world every year, always features leading, cutting-edge experts to talk about health, finance, and the state of the world.

She said, "I couldn't help noticing the theme and desire that was behind their selection of speakers. These very, very rich people want to know how they can control things—control their health, control the economy, control politics. I almost wanted to stand up and shout, 'But we are not in control. Don't you get it? No amount of information or insight is going to change that fact!'"

It reminds me of a joke circulating on the Internet about the number of very upset health-conscious people who will eventually have to face the fact that they died of "nothing."

When Paul said that "all things work together for good for those who love God, who are called according to his purpose" (Rom. 8:28 NRSV), he was reminding us that if we ask, God will indeed hold the ladder for us as we make our way toward the goal.

Jesus showed us how to walk the ladder. He did it standing straight up, and he did it on his knees. And in the Garden of Gethsemane, when his mind was begging him to take the easier way, Jesus showed us that spiritual balance doesn't come from your head—it comes from the midst of you—the midst of you that we commonly refer to as "guts."

Jesus held the ladder.

QUESTIONS

1. What "pirate's ladder" are you facing?

2. Are you trying to do it alone?

3. Have you asked Jesus to hold the ladder for you?

4. Do you trust him to do that?

5. Can you still trust him to help you, even when you flip over and fall?

6. Where does your "balance" come from?

Dear Lord,
Thank you for holding the ladder for me. Give me the guts to keep climbing this challenging ladder you have placed in front of me. And help me remember that, no matter how many times I flip over or fall, all of your life, all of my life, is by your design. Amen.

DO SUCCESSION
PLANNING

THIS NIGHT THY SOUL SHALL
BE REQUIRED OF THEE.
—LUKE 12:20

With a majority of CEOs being in their late fifties to early sixties, succession planning is of paramount importance to organizations large and small. I have spoken with numerous people in key board positions at large companies, and their major concern is getting the CEOs to start grooming successors. When a person has proven himself or herself in the capacity of leadership, that person may personally be sailing along in his or her prime, not wanting to face mortality.

In the wake of 9/11, we all are more painfully aware of how precious and temporary life is. Yet have we taken the vital steps necessary to name and, more important, groom our successors?

If the name of your game is "Get to the Top and Stay There," then you have very short-range (and wishful) thinking. If we are indeed but a gleam of sunlight on a drop of water in the ocean of humanity, what wave are we riding? How have we planned for our death and what follows?

My mother was the beneficiary of my father's foresight and planning regarding his mortality. His insurance policy was such that when he died suddenly of a heart attack, my mother was able to move into her retirement with few financial worries. Yet amazingly a huge percentage of people in this country die without a will, leaving their successors and heirs and assigns expensive and emotionally exhausting messes to clean up. According to *Consumer Reports* magazine, seven out of ten Americans die without a will. Financial author and radio talk show host Dave Ramsey says, "Look, you know you're going to die. So get a will!"

In a screenplay writing course I took we were taught that in order to heighten interest and drama, there must be some kind of deadline that the main character is facing. If each of us could look our own "deadline" in the face and realize that there *is* one, perhaps we would take more dramatic actions toward our succession planning.

Jesus began his succession planning almost from day

one. Knowing that his time on earth was short, he began telling his followers that they would not always have him, and that they needed to pay attention to what he was doing, and how, so that when he left, they could do even greater things. He told them: "Most assuredly, I say to you, he who believes in Me, the works that I do he will do also; and greater works than these he will do . . . that the Father may be glorified in the Son (John 14:12–13 NKJV).

While Jesus was still walking the earth, he consciously and pointedly gave the keys to his kingdom to Peter, naming him his representative. He also commissioned the apostles to be his voice and hands and feet on earth (Matt. 28:19–20).

From the cross he named John the Beloved as his successor in the family: "John, this is your new mother. Mother, this is your new son." With his dying breath he was demonstrating the importance of taking care of those who are left behind.

Some of us never think beyond our own worlds or our own infinitely fascinating kingdom or queendom. Garrison Keillor asks, "How many narcissists does it take to screw in a lightbulb?" The answer is: "Only one. He or she just stands on a ladder and holds the bulb while the world revolves around them." (This reminds me of a bumper sticker I saw the other day: "If you are taken in the Rapture, can I have your car?" Here is someone wanting to be on the receiving end of succession planning.)

Comedian Jerry Seinfeld stated in an interview that he never really knew he had feelings until his first daughter was born. After revealing this unusual and amazingly sentimental side of himself, he then recovered by joking, "Of course, you have to realize that babies are meant for only one thing—to replace you!"

If you are a parent or a grandparent, you are already inclined to think about succession planning. But the succession planning I am talking about here is twofold. One fold has to do with, Whom are you going to leave behind and with what legacy? The other fold is, What kind of life are you preparing for *yourself* on the other side?

In Luke 12, verses 16 through 21, Jesus told the story about a man who was doing very well in business:

> The ground of a certain rich man yielded plentifully. And he thought within himself, saying, "What shall I do, since I have no room to store my crops?" So he said, "I will do this: I will pull down my barns and build greater, and there I will store all my crops and my goods. And I will say to my soul, 'Soul, you have many goods laid up for many years; take your ease; eat, drink, and be merry.'" But God said to him, "Fool! This night your soul will be required of you; then whose will those things be which you have provided?" So is he who lays up treasure for himself, and is not rich toward God. (NKJV)

No big barn is going to do you any good when the *spiritual* weighing scales come up, and only your heart goes on it.

Not long ago I spoke at the Christian Management Association Meeting. I was able to attend a number of the other sessions before giving my speech, and I was blessed to hear from a young man who is totally convinced that his bank account lies in heaven, not here. He and his wife have chosen to live in a simple, three-bedroom house in a nice but modest neighborhood while they have donated several million dollars to a project they believe in. He said, "God said the multiple in heaven is ten times whatever you have, so my wife and I are busy building our retirement account in the place we intend to live the longest!" I loved and needed his perspective. This twosome practiced wise succession planning. They were lining their beds in heaven, not on earth, and Jesus said that was a good thing to do.

Jesus will have you think carefully about your succession planning.

QUESTIONS

1. What legacy are you leaving behind to others in terms of "soul work"?

2. How much planning are you doing for your life on the other side?

Dear Lord,

I am so caught up in trying to lay up my riches on earth rather than in heaven. Help me think about whom and what I will leave behind, and what I am laying a foundation for in heaven. Make me ever mindful of how temporary and fleeting is this dream of a life. Amen.

HAVE TO

JUSTIFY

NO LONGER

LET YOUR "YES" BE YES
AND YOUR "NO" BE NO.
—JAMES 5:12 (NRSV)

When the apostle James wrote, "Let your 'Yes' be yes and your 'No' be no," he was teaching several important concepts. The most obvious, and the one that I was always taught, was the importance of keeping your word, or having integrity.

The one I want to talk about is the habit of justification

that so many of us use to our detriment. Oftentimes, where there is a multiplication of words, there is a lack of clarity and purpose. If you don't believe me, read statements by politicians. They seem to cover all the bases while never quite making it home with their points. The object of the game seems to be keeping your attention on them while they appear intelligent and informed, yet never letting you really know what they are thinking, perhaps because they don't even know.

So, one weakness of justification is that there is a multiplication of words around what should be a clear communication. "I did this because . . ." can quickly turn into some form of excuse. And the longer the tail, the easier the animal is to catch.

My mentor Catherine Calhoun taught me the value of role-playing difficult conversations or situations to gain clarity around intent. Many were the days when we walked the riverbank of the Rio Grande, role-playing with each other situations ranging from asking for a raise to turning in a resignation.

Recently I counseled a corporate board member who had come to the conclusion that one of the company's vice presidents needed to be fired. There had been turmoil and distrust in the company for more than a year, and the vice president, who was the board member's personal friend, had taken a hard and arrogant stance—justifying his every mistake and refusing to listen to reason. This board member told me early in the coaching session that he was lying awake, with his stomach in knots, dreading the conversation that needed to happen. I volunteered to be the recalcitrant vice president, and he launched into his "firing" speech. His conversation went something like this:

> BOARD MEMBER: Sam, I asked you to join me today because I want to talk about the future of our company and your role in it.
>
> VICE PRESIDENT (*me*): Well, you know that nothing is more on my heart than the future of the company.
>
> BOARD MEMBER: You know that this past year and a half has been very difficult for all of us. We don't want to repeat the mistakes of the past.
>
> VICE PRESIDENT: No, we certainly don't. You know, between the two of us, Eric, I am glad that the new board elections are coming up. This last group was so stubborn and hard that I couldn't get any of my new ideas through to them. I sure will be glad when we get a whole new team that is open to my ideas.
>
> BOARD MEMBER: Sam, I don't think there will be a whole new crop coming up. What I want to know is, what new behaviors do you intend to display that will keep the mistakes of last year from happening?
>
> VICE PRESIDENT: As I told you, I know that I made a few errors. But this is a team effort, and I can't be responsible for taking on everyone's shortcomings.

At that point I stopped the conversation and asked the board member if he really thought the vice president could display new behaviors that would salvage his job.

He said, "No."

Then I asked him why he was going down that conversational track with him, making him think that there was something "fixable" he could do.

He replied, "Well, I was trying not to be rude."

"You let him take the lead in the conversation, didn't you?" I asked.

"Yes, I did," he admitted. "And your words sounded so much like what he would say that I just fell into trying to reason with him."

I asked, "Are you clear that the vice president needs to go?"

"Yes," he said. "Without a doubt."

"Then why are you leaving room for doubt to enter into the conversation?" I asked. "He will try to justify his way into keeping the job, and you are trying to justify why, in a roundabout way, he isn't doing the job and needs to go. All this justification only leads to obfuscation, and in my dictionary, *obfuscation* means 'muddy water,' not 'living water.'"

"You're right," said the board member.

"Let's try again," I said, "but this time I'll be you and you be the vice president."

"Okay," he said. "Let's do it."

BOARD MEMBER (*me*): Sam, this is a very difficult meeting for me because you and I have been friends for a long time. As you know, this past year and a half has been filled with a great deal of turmoil in our company, and it doesn't seem to be getting better. The board called an emergency session last night and unfortunately gave you a vote of "no confidence." The decision is that you will be given twenty-four hours to respond with a resignation, or we will be forced to terminate you.

VICE PRESIDENT: (*speechless*)

BOARD MEMBER: I know this is a blow for you, but I am praying that in the long run you will see that it was best for all concerned. I'll be in my office all day, and I'll be expecting your response by this time tomorrow.

VICE PRESIDENT: Well, I guess I have no choice . . . Some friend you turned out to be.

BOARD MEMBER: Sam, this was a unanimous board decision made for what we feel is best for the company. I will still be your friend.

You will note that in this conversation, the board member, who was the initiator, took the lead and gave fact after fact rather than weak justifications or invitations to hobble down an already worn-out trail. This was not a dialogue about relationship building or trying to gain understanding.

This was a case where the facts were clear, the decision had been made, and there was no turning back for either party. Can you see how the first conversation might have gone on indefinitely with the board member feeling more and more sidetracked and frustrated, and the vice president taking the lead in the merry-go-round?

My next role-play was with a woman who dreaded to tell her doctor that she had gotten a second opinion on her decision that she needed back surgery, and she was going to opt for traditional conservative care instead. She had seen her lose her temper with other patients and had witnessed her "firing" a patient who dared to disagree with her.

Betty said, "I am so afraid to talk to her! What if she fires me too?"

"Well, it's your body that is going to be cut open, not hers, so you have total authority and final decision-making capacity." I asked her if there was anything she could do or say that would make her change her mind.

"No," she said. "My mind is made up."

"Okay, let's role-play," I said. "Hit it. You be the patient, and I'll be the doctor."

> BETTY: Doctor Richards, could you tell me again why you think I need back surgery?
> DOCTOR (*me*): I told you already, Mrs. Taylor, that the tests show that you are a prime candidate for this procedure.

BETTY: Might there be a reason for me *not* to have the surgery?

DOCTOR (*voice rising*): Mrs. Taylor, I already told you my diagnosis. If you don't like what I have to say, you can go somewhere else.

BETTY (*voice getting softer*): Well, I was just wondering . . .

At that point Betty admitted that she was getting scared and could feel her chest constricting at the prospect of facing her doctor's anger.

We did a new role-play, and I took her role.

ME (*as Betty*): Doctor Richards, I have greatly appreciated so much you being my doctor for the last few years, and I really admire the work that you do. As you know, I do not want back surgery. I took the test results to another physician who specializes in spinal care. He said that the tests were inconclusive and that this could be treated with standard, conservative care. I need to ask you now if you will partner with me in this approach. If you cannot see your way clear to do that, I will understand, and I thank you for everything you have done for me to this point.

DOCTOR: You have a right to a second opinion. If you choose alternatives that I feel are not wise, I must ask you to find another doctor.

ME: I figured you might feel that way. Thank you again for all your help. Good-bye.

After that role-play Betty could see that she needed to take the lead in the conversation and state clearly, without detailed or weak-kneed justification, her decision about her own body. Interestingly enough, when the actual conversation took place, Dr. Richards immediately agreed that, in fact, she did *not* need the operation. All of Betty's reasoning and justifications became unnecessary once she got clear about her truth.

Jesus said the truth will set us free. When you know what the truth is, you are called upon to speak it clearly and without justification.

Another reason to avoid justification is that people who are manipulative by nature often intentionally keep people talking so they can insert a phrase or sentence that will lead the conversation into the area *they* want it to go. Remember, the shorter your tail (or tale), the less likely you are to get caught in a trap.

Jesus didn't stand and justify who he was before his accusers. He never gave a lengthy, detailed explanation about who he was or what he did. He just did it. He just "was."

"Let your 'Yes' be yes and your 'No' be no." Those who learn how to do this move forward faster because they move in the power of the truth.

QUESTIONS

1. When and where do you find yourself justifying your actions? Would you say that this is a sign of strength or weakness?

2. Spend the next few days noticing when and where people begin to justify or obscure their actions and thoughts. What might be their motives?

3. Once you have sought wisdom around an issue and made up your mind, experiment for the next week not justifying your actions, but simply letting them stand, because you do.

Dear Lord,
Help me to be more clear in my decisions and my decision-making capability. Help me not give those who would manipulate or deceive any extra or unnecessary words to use against me. Amen.

BE GIVEN

NEW PERSPECTIVES

AND GOD WILL WIPE AWAY EVERY TEAR FROM THEIR
EYES; THERE SHALL BE NO MORE DEATH, NOR
SORROW, NOR CRYING. THERE SHALL BE NO MORE
PAIN, FOR THE FORMER THINGS HAVE PASSED AWAY.
—REVELATION 21:4 (NKJV)

Jo invited me along to take her five-year-old son, Donny,
to the Oasis Water Park. It was an unusually warm winter
day in Phoenix, and we were determined to "hit the water"
and enjoy the sunshine together. After a luxurious swim,
filled with much splashing and laughter by little Donny, we
went together to the large heated spa.

While Jo and I visited, little Donny climbed out right beside us, then turned suddenly and jumped feet first into the water, narrowly missing the third step that jutted out at the bottom of the spa.

We both yelled in alarm, but it was too late. He floated to the top in a limp bubblelike position as we and the lifeguard lunged into the water to help him.

Jo reached him first, touching his back gently. He lifted up his head with his face all dripping wet and then acted shocked to find three worried-looking adults huddled around him. "What were you doing?" asked Jo. "You frightened us badly!"

He said, "I was trying to make a human bubble."

Jo continued in her relieved but now teaching tone: "Donny, how many times have I told you not to jump off the edge of the pool!"

She was about to launch into the second phase of her lecture when he looked up at her with his innocent brown eyes and said, "Mommy, if you were a bird, what would you be seeing right now?"

Her eyes widened in surprise as she contemplated his question, suddenly transforming from an angry and lecturing adult to an eagle soaring above the scene.

Jo and I later laughed at his childish wisdom and ability to change the subject. Yet it made me think of how Jesus dealt with people who were entangled in appearances of reality but were forgetting the bigger picture.

Jesus looked at the little girl who lay ashen and still on her bed. "She is not dead; she's sleeping," he said calmly. Here he offered the family a change of perspective that led to a different outcome.

"Tear this temple down and in three days I will raise it up again," he said. Here he offered a change of perspective on the temporality of life and the power the people felt they had to permanently destroy it.

When I attended the Executive Summit meeting of the International Coaching Federation, there was much discussion around this topic: When and how is coaching really leadership development? A leader's job is, first of all, to change the perspective on a situation. A coach's job is to do the same.

"Perception equals reality" is a phrase I learned in my Marketing 101 class in college. It holds true in virtually every human endeavor. Psychologists have documented the fact that it is not the actual events that harm us, so much as the perception of the events.

In the stunning movie *Life Is Beautiful* a father finds himself and his young son thrown into a concentration camp in Germany during World War Two. Trying to shield his son from the horror of their situation, he tells the boy that it is all a game, and the first one who gets scared, loses. Somehow he is able to continually convince the boy that none of the cruelty they are seeing is real, but only a play that is taking place. He even predicts the ending, saying at the end of the game a big tank with smiling men is going to come into the camp and declare the winner. When indeed the tank of the Americans pulls into camp, the little boy runs leaping and yelling in joy to greet it: "We won! We won!" The father's change of perception shielded the child from immense mental and emotional harm.

Jesus does the same for us. When he says that "every tear shall be wiped away," he is teaching us that somehow we are in a play that is going to have a happy ending, no matter what it looks like now.

You may be smack dab up against the hardest stone and biggest step of your life, thinking that you do not have the strength or skill set necessary to overcome it.

Yet Jesus, your Life Coach, is standing right beside you, saying, "Beloved, how would you look at this problem if you knew you could fly?"

QUESTIONS

1. What situation are you facing right now that has you all tied up in knots?

2. How do you think a bird might view your situation?

3. How can you help others gain a new perspective when they are facing seemingly insurmountable difficulties?

Dear Lord,

You said we were made of spirit, not flesh. Help me remember to keep the spiritual perspective on all my trials, knowing that you are beside me, and you see and know the happy ending that is mine. Amen.

HEAR

OUTRAGEOUS

REQUESTS

WHOEVER BELIEVES IN ME
WILL PERFORM THE SAME
WORKS AS I DO MYSELF,
AND WILL PERFORM EVEN GREATER WORKS.
—JOHN 14:12 (NJB)

I don't know how anyone attempting to follow Jesus could ever be bored. As author Anne Dillard says, if we truly knew who we were worshiping, we'd all be wearing hard hats in church.

Jesus came not to reinforce your comfort zone, but to set your old small-minded ways on fire.

He doesn't ask you to just take a step here or there—he asks you to leap tall buildings in a single bound. His requests will cause you to leave behind maybe everything that you thought you knew.

Jesus went from the fetal position to living and dying full out—with arms outstretched as wide as they could go—and he asks the same of you and me.

He also said, "Whosoever shall seek to save his life shall lose it" (Luke 17:33). In other words, if you try to preserve your ego identity, your time on earth will be wasted and empty. But if you are willing to give up the ground of everything you think you know, and follow the way that he will show you, you will be given blessings beyond your wildest imaginings.

According to my friend Doug Hall, author of *Meaningful Marketing* (Betterway Publications, 2003), most people automatically reject new ideas when first presented to them. It is only after hearing the ideas repeatedly do the concepts begin to seem possible. And after a little bit more exposure to the ideas they begin to seem not only possible, but *necessary*. God indeed has outrageous ideas for you that may, in fact, be vitally necessary for you.

I have been blessed in being able to often help people discern their divine purpose in life. I am continually amazed at how suddenly and radically a life can change when a person heeds God's outrageous requests. In this laboratory that is my life I have seen priests transformed into ski instructors, CEOs turned into youth pastors, and youth pastors become CEOs. I have seen housewives become juried artists, prisoners become bread makers, students become preachers, nurses become mothers, lawyers become wine makers, and CPAs turned into distributors of cookies at day care centers. And *loving* it.

It is one thing to ask God for what you want. Real change happens when you ask what God wants for you.

That's when transformation occurs.

Just think about the transformations that took place all around Jesus of Nazareth.

He turned fishermen into fishers of souls, outcast woment into honored heroines, tax collectors into counselors, physicians into poets, and murderers into church leaders.

Jesus took the bread and broke it, and about five thousand were fed that day. Jesus will take the bread of your life and ask simply, "May I break this with you?" If you nod and say, "Yes," you will be multiplied in ways you never dreamed of (or you can just keep your sticky old Spam sandwich).

QUESTIONS

1. What outrageous requests is Jesus, your Coach, making of you?

2. What if what he's asking really could come true?

3. What if the only thing keeping it from happening is you?

4. What would happen if you released the brake and decided to go for the ride?

Dear Lord,
You are the builder of roads and the knower of roads. Help me trust you—just to simply trust you and say "Yes," when you say, "Let's go!" Amen.

RESPECT

YOUR FRAGILE

THINGS

MY HOUSE WAS DESIGNATED A
HOUSE OF PRAYER FOR THE NATIONS;
YOU'VE TURNED IT INTO A
HANGOUT FOR THIEVES.
—MARK 11:17 *(THE MESSAGE)*

With more than one million frequent flier miles to my name, I have had a great deal of time to ponder an airplane's anatomy. Whenever I am seated over the wing, I look with some amusement and no small amount of prayer at the letters placed outside over a small section of the wing. The letters read: "Do Not Step Here." My prayer is that nobody has. Obviously that small movable part on the huge metal airship is fragile. One misstep could cause enough damage to bring the whole plane tumbling down.

What many of us fail to realize is that we have within us areas of the soul that also have the same lettering: "Do Not Step Here." Yet somehow, mostly through our own neglect, we allow others to trample all over our "fragile pieces," and then we wonder why we don't seem to have the energy we need to get off the ground.

People who are in service to others, and especially those who are Christians, often believe that they must give all they have all the time to all who ask wherever they may ask it. I am reminded of the cartoonist Gary Larson's illustration of the Boneless Chicken Ranch. His drawing shows a cluster of lost-looking chickens unable to stand or lift up their heads, flopping around like so many scattered throw rugs.

Jesus was very intentional about his work. He did not heal all of the people in Jerusalem. He did not raise all of the dead. He knew his mission, and he stuck to it. He was also very conscious about his boundaries.

In the morning when Mary saw Jesus after his resurrection, he told her, "Do not touch me." Yet later, that very same afternoon, he allowed Thomas to plunge his hands into his wounds. Part of guarding your fragile things is recognizing when and where and how to raise and lower your personal boundaries at appropriate times.

When I first began conducting our two-day Path Training Seminars, I was amazed at how intense the energy was that was flowing out of me toward the people in the group. In a room covered by prayer and filled with people who were acutely interested in discerning God's will for their lives, it was amazing to see how the Holy Spirit worked through laughter and tears and life-changing, pattern-shattering revelations.

Anyone who has ever led a group of this kind knows that to stay fully focused on the person or people in front of you, you have to drop your shields, filters, and barriers so that the Holy Spirit can flow and guide you.

What I failed to realize was how fragile a state it left me in the day after the seminars were over. Thinking that I could simply move from that Friday-through-Sunday experience into a full workweek on Monday, I learned through a number of costly mistakes that I needed to take time apart to allow my cup to be refilled, or I had nothing (not even common sense) to give. My very energetic relationship with God could not be sustained at that level without my taking time apart, alone, in order to be refilled.

Jesus did the same thing. He took time regularly to draw apart, pray, and be refilled for the very draining work that he was to do each day. His fragile thing was his unique, intense, one-on-one relationship with God the Father, and he did not let others trample on or barge into or interrupt that time.

When he overturned the tables of the money changers in the temple, Jesus said in anger, "My Father's house is a house of prayer, but you have turned it into a den of thieves" (my paraphrase, Matt. 21:13). He knew that this connection—the fragile thing of prayer—needed to be nurtured and guarded and tended each day. When I read this scripture passage again, I wondered where I have and let thieves set up their tables and begin to haggle with me, keeping me, in effect, from entering my relationship with God.

Prayer time, meditation time, alone time—this is one way to guard and respect your fragile things. Jesus taught us to respect that or else we cannot fly.

QUESTIONS

1. What would you say is your most fragile thing in your life?

2. Who or what is stepping on it?

3. Why have you been allowing that to happen?

4. What could be the consequences of your not reclaiming it?

5. Imagine what your life can be when you allow your fragile thing the time and space it needs.

Dear Lord,

You created me with a need for you. When I am apart from you, I can do nothing—no matter how busy I may seem. Call me back to the fragile place—the sacred space of us—those intense breath-to-breath moments when just you and I are together. Amen.

HAVE SOME

BAD HAIR

DAYS

GOD ORDAINED THAT A WORM SHOULD ATTACK
THE CASTOR-OIL PLANT—AND IT WITHERED.
—JONAH 4:7 (NJB)

Jonah was in despair. The doom he had prophesied to Nineveh had been averted because the people actually listened and repented.

Jonah went off to mope, and a castor oil tree gave him shade.

But the next day the very God who had ordained that it

grow ordained that a worm should destroy it. God needed to make a point to Jonah that *he* was in control and had a right to change his mind.

If there is one thing that many of us desire in these chaotic and uncertain times, it is order. The case has been made that radical fundamentalism rises when there seems to be nothing definite to hang on to. Black-and-white thinking, rules that cannot be broken, "my way or the highway" certainty brings a kind of comfort to people who have low tolerance for the creativity that can come from chaos.

Political thinkers who today want most to adhere to the Constitution would be considered conservatives by almost any rule of thumb. Yet those who created the Constitution were actually radical change artists who in their time were considered by many as being "off the charts" liberals. "You want us to take away the power of the monarchy and give it to the common people? You must be crazy!" It was out of utter chaos and confusion that our country was created. It was out of chaos and darkness that *the universe* was created. Yet how often we tend to forget that.

People who believe that God is frozen in stone are either ignoring or forgetting the radical, messy, "thinking on your feet and with your heart" style of leadership that Jesus embodied.

Jesus was born in a cave, not in a palace. He was placed not on fine linens, but on straw. He was surrounded not by physicians, but by shepherds and immigrants.

He grew up poor—or at least no wealthier than middle class. He did not fit the pictures of magnificence he was supposed to. And then, to top it off, he hung out with sinners, tax collectors, disabled people, and fishermen (not the group a mother would probably choose for her firstborn son). Christ was quite comfortable with chaos. In fact he seemed to create it everywhere he went. As my grandfather used to say with a smile, "He created a stir wherever he went":

+ Turning over the tables in the temple.

+ Turning water into wine at a wedding.

+ Talking to a woman shunned by society.

+ Boiling down the Torah to a single sentence.

+ Healing a man on the Sabbath.

+ Praising a woman for "wasting" expensive perfume.

+ Rebuking religious leaders for their hardness of heart.

+ Setting prisoners free.

+ Turning ashes into beauty.

+ Turning mourning robes into wedding dresses.

The list goes on and on.

When people thought Jesus should have zigged, he zagged. Just when they thought they had him figured out, he would surprise them and head in another direction. Was it madness, as members of his own family feared? Or was there, underneath and suffusing it all, a divine faith that could be seen only when viewed from above?

I had the privilege of spending time with Mike Yaconelli, the owner and founder of Youth Specialties, an organization that serves youth directors nationwide. Mike had a passion for youth directors, having been one himself. So twenty-five years ago he decided to have a gathering for youth directors in a nice hotel instead of a rundown camp "so that they would see they are just as valued as business-people." Today Youth Specialties reaches more than twelve thousand youth directors across the country—encouraging them and equipping them to serve their very special charges.

At the particular meeting where I met Mike, we were in Nashville in the Green Room. I was about to go on stage and address five thousand interdenominational youth direc-tors, who had just been entertained by a hip-hop band and a Christian comedian. It was not my usual "opening act." In those brief few minutes Mike and I bonded. He said, "I hope you realize you may be ruining your reputation by hanging out with us." I laughed and said, "I hope so."

Turns out Mike and his wife lived on a houseboat in San Diego part time, and then he pastored what he called "the slowest growing church in America" when not on the road serving youth leaders. Mike gifted me with a copy of his lat-est book *Messy Spirituality*, and I devoured it on the plane ride home.

In it Mike tells the story of a young girl who carefully and slowly made her way up to the altar. The Bible was laid open for her, and she began to recite with every fiber of her being the scripture passage for that particular Sunday.

She had asked the pastor for months if she could do it, and he had encouraged her. She had studied and practiced endlessly in her room, and she had eagerly awaited the special day. What the angels heard and saw was a heart pouring itself out to God in joy and celebration. What the board members of the congregation heard and saw was a girl with cerebral palsy slowly and haltingly working to mouth every word. The two-verse passage took her fifteen minutes to complete. When she finished, she turned with triumph to the pastor, who smiled and gave her an enthusiastic thumbs-up. Tears were streaming down both of their faces.

Immediately following the service, the furious chairman and finance officer of the board were waiting for the pastor in his study. They berated him and threatened to have him fired for offending and insulting the congregation with that embarrassing display: "You will have readers who know how to read the scripture, and you will get this service finished on time, or you are out of here, you understand?" The pastor, shocked at their display, simply nodded.

The following day he resigned. That pastor was Mike's father.

You see, Mike and his father before him—and I and my

mother, too—believe that God loves us even in and through our messiness. The subtitle of Mike's book is *God's Annoying Love for Imperfect People*. That sort of says it all, doesn't it, when it comes to Jesus?

We usually acknowledge our own imperfection. But we forget sometimes that God is annoying, too.

Author Anne Lamott described Jesus as a cat that kept following her, refusing to be shooed away. Paul would without a doubt have chosen something other than being knocked off his donkey as a way of getting a message. Mary certainly couldn't have been pleased when Jesus refused to come when she called him.

God's love is sometimes annoying. Things will not always go according to your plans.

I have a friend named Belle who is very unconventional in her ways and actions with people. One particular friend of ours named Chris, who is rather compulsive about his closets and drawers, often will be fuming when Belle leaves one of his parties, because Chris inevitably finds all his clothes messed up and his closets rearranged just for fun by Belle. What an annoying friend to have! Yet Chris needs Belle in his life almost as much as he needs anyone. For Belle is sent to teach him that life can be messy sometimes, and it is okay. Love is still there. Love still survives.

Jesus loved to laugh, loved to throw unconventional parties full of messy and unconventional people. Aren't you glad that you and I are invited, too?

(Having a bad hair day? Maybe Jesus just rubbed your head.)

QUESTIONS

1. Where in your life are you trying to avoid chaos?

2. Where might God be in the midst of it?

3. What does the term *messy spirituality* mean to you?

4. Do you think Mike's father was right or wrong to do what he did?

5. How might you have reacted if you were in the congregation?

6. When has Jesus messed up your hair?

Dear Lord,
Things don't always go the way I want them to. Help me realize that your divine and loving order is behind and underneath it all. And that you sometimes might mess up my hair just to say, "Loosen up. I love you." Amen.

LEAVE REGRET
BEHIND

ONCE THE HAND IS LAID ON THE PLOUGH,
NO ONE WHO LOOKS BACK IS FIT
FOR THE KINGDOM OF GOD.
—LUKE 9:62 (NJB)

Perhaps one of the most oft-quoted sayings I heard this year was, "Don't die with the music still in you."

When Jesus called out to the fishermen, "Follow me, and I will make you fishers of men," he was saying, "Follow me, and you will live a life free of regrets. Follow me, and you will live all the music that is in you."

As a child, I was haunted by the notion that I would die

without the people I loved knowing that I loved them. Whether this intense desire to express my feelings came from the daily drills we were doing in school, diving under our desks to avoid nuclear attack, or whether it was the Welsh blood in me that my grandmother declared was full of the poet's muse, I am not sure. But I do know that starting around the age of ten, I began to write love poems and notes and cards in earnest. (Several years ago my mother hauled out ten huge boxes of cards and notes I have sent her over the years. She smiled and said, "Honey, I think I got your point. You love me. Now, what do you want to do with these? I'm running out of space.")

My friend and mentor Catherine Calhoun and I once observed in amazement how often people would burst into tears around us. The quality that Catherine and I have in common, which is perhaps the one that causes tears in others, is that we love to ask, "If all things were possible, what would you be doing with your life?" She has had pastors, CEOs, and bellboys choke up at this inquiry, and I have shaped a career out of asking this question a thousand ways.

It is God's desire to see tigers be tigers, and lambs be lambs, and not have one think it must be the other. Never before in the history of the world has a civilization been more capable of living fully expressed and developed lives, yet the statistics are still staggering that we are not.

America imprisons more of its population than any other country in the world, except Russia. So much for the notion that the land of the brave is also the land of the free. Freedom can come only from within, and Jesus was adamant about teaching that concept. We create our own prisons. We shut ourselves behind bars of our own making. Jesus hands us the key, but we are the only ones who can use it.

In an interview with pop singer Whitney Houston, Diane Sawyer asked, "So which of these drugs was the demon for you? Crack? Cocaine? Heroin?" Whitney looked at her for a moment and then said, "None of them was the demon. I was. I had the freedom to choose."

Regrets are about things we wish we had done differently. Yet I believe that if we just take time to sit and project into the future a little bit, we can shape a life that is free of regret.

Carl Jung once said, "Nothing affects the life of a child so much as the unlived life of its parent." You would not believe how this phenomenon of "unlived lives" is revealed to have shaped so much of our own existence. Take a moment right now for yourself, and identify what was your father's or your mother's unlived life. Once you identify it, you might see how much of your own life has been shaped by that regret . . . by the things your parent wanted, but was unable to do. Perhaps it was circumstances that caused both parents to have unlived lives. But perhaps it was choices they made, or failed to make, that kept them from fulfillment.

Taking that into the future, what "unlived life" are you facing?

Jesus talked about this when he said, in essence, "Don't go out and build a bigger barn. Go out and build a bigger life."

QUESTIONS

1. Based on your life up to this point, what are your regrets?

2. Based on your life going forward, what might your regrets be?

3. Name three actions you are going to take today to make sure that doesn't happen.

Dear Lord,
You did not die with the music still in you. Help me do the same. Amen.

HONOR YOUR
ANCESTORS

HONOUR YOUR FATHER AND YOUR MOTHER SO
THAT YOU MAY LIVE LONG IN THE LAND.
—EXODUS 20:12 (NJB)

Not long ago I was disembarking from a three-hour flight to Chicago. The plane had been significantly delayed taking off, and people were anxious to make their next connections. However, the flight attendant selected a frail, elderly woman to exit the plane first and helped lead her down the walkway. The woman's pace was slow and measured as she carefully placed her cane in front of her, one step at a time. I could sense the desire of the crowd behind me, wanting to rush past this woman of slow step and old age. But strangely enough, none of us did. I remember thinking, *It is right for us to walk slowly sometimes and pace ourselves according to those who have gone before us*.

I was shocked when I read a statement that our Western culture is the only one that blames, rather than honors, our ancestors. It has become *de rigueur* to blame our illnesses and psychoses on our poor, pitiful parents, who either ignored or coddled us, pushed or delayed us, gave us bad examples, abandoned or overprotected us. "Freud did a disservice to humanity when he laid a foundation that basically everything is the mother's fault," said a therapist friend while we lunched on salad. As she casually reached for her package of cigarettes she added, "I probably wouldn't be addicted to this stuff if my mother hadn't smoked so much while she was pregnant with me."

While it is wise to examine the patterns of our parents' behaviors, both negative and positive, ultimately we do ourselves a favor when we are able to bless and honor them, somehow, some way.

The fifth of the Ten Commandments is: Honor thy father and mother that you may live long in the land. It is the only commandment with a guaranteed blessing attached to it.

Jesus honored his mother when he saw to it from the cross that she would be taken care of after his death. "John, this is your new mother now. Mother, this is your new son," he said in his final hours as his life ebbed away from him.

Honoring your father and mother doesn't mean that you have no boundaries with them. Jesus set a boundary with his mother when she wanted him to come and talk to her, perhaps delaying him from his work (Mark 3:31–35 NKJV). In that instance, he declined her request, saying that his family included "whoever does the will of God." Yet the Bible also tells us that he grew in wisdom and favor with his parents, listened to their lessons, and learned them well (Luke 2:52).

I think that this culture has driven us away from honoring those who loved and raised us. Our almost narcissistic self-involvement has also caused us to actually blame our ancestors for all that they *didn't* do for us.

Comedienne Roseanne used to joke to her complaining television children, "Look, I got you here alive, didn't I? That's where my responsibility ends."

I was delighted to read in a *People* magazine article about a man who bought a nursing home in a small town and renovated it to combine it with a preschool. Now, every child is paired with a "grandparent," and there is even a petting zoo on the premises so the elderly can still enjoy the companionship of furry friends.

The owner said, "I looked around at nursing homes and realized that the goal had simply been absence from pain. But that isn't enough. Life means there is the presence of joy, and I intended to bring that to them."

I also believe that nearly everything that happens in the news is a metaphor for the condition of our collective human spirit. For instance, we were shocked when a woman was found to have left two preschoolers at home alone while she went off to chase a new boyfriend she had met through the Internet. The kids were left to fend for themselves for two weeks until a neighbor noticed that the mail had been uncollected, and she then became concerned and called the police. As the mother was being led away in handcuffs, a reporter asked her what she would say to her children. She said, "I would tell them that I am a bad mother, but I love them dearly." How enraged I became at that woman's neglect! Yet as I sat back and looked at what her story tells about us, I realized that as a society, we are often like that woman—leaving our children neglected and unattended while we chase after the elusive happiness promised through the glitter and shine of technology.

Ray Anderson, CEO of Interface, told a story once when he spoke in Santa Fe about the time when he became adamant that his textile manufacturing firm become totally earth friendly in its policies—looking for every possible way to reduce pollution. He recalled that some of his employees said, "What's up with Ray and his new 'earth' kick? Has he gone around the bend?" Ray leaned forward as he delivered his speech and said in carefully measured words, "Yes, indeed I have. I have gone around the bend and seen what is there if we do not change our ways. And I am going to spend the rest of my life here ensuring that my children, and their children, have a green earth to play in."

A theologian recently wrote that we must go from "heavenly purple to earthly green" in our thinking—no longer claiming dominance over the world, but respect for it.

Respect. And honor. We must honor those who came before us, or we cannot move forward. And we must honor those who will follow us by living centered and earth-friendly ways.

Jesus honored his mother even from the cross, making sure that she was taken care of. And he lived his life with every breath, trying to do the will of his Father. Jesus did not blame his ancestors for his problems. Neither must we.

QUESTIONS

1. How are you honoring your mother and your father?

2. What is the difference between boundary setting and honoring?

3. Why is it important to walk slowly sometimes in the footsteps of those who have gone before?

4. Whom are you blaming for your problems today?

5. If you shifted from blame to wonder, which ancestor would you take to "show-and-tell" and why?

Dear Lord,
You created me from a multitude of possible DNA strands. Thank you. And thank you for choosing perfect ancestors for me—those who could show me what I need to learn in this life so that I may serve you more. Amen.

NOT LORD IT
OVER OTHERS

HE POURED WATER INTO A BASIN AND
BEGAN TO WASH THE DISCIPLES' FEET.
—JOHN 13:5 (NRSV)

As a consultant to corporations and organizations in various sizes and layers of society, I read the headlines daily to keep informed of what is happening in the world of business. Perhaps like you, I have been stunned by the arrogance and sheer ignorance of some of the moves made by very powerful and well-paid executives.

One recent example will no doubt go in the record

books as a huge blunder in public relations. For the purposes of education, not judgment, let's look at what happened with American Airlines.

I remember being on a flight where the stewardesses were huddled in the galley, discussing what they were going to do. The headlines the next day gave insight to my observation. "Fate of American Hinges on Flight Attendants" read the news in bold print. The fine print revealed that the pilots' union and the machinists' union had agreed to significant wage cuts. The only group that was still undecided was the union of the flight attendants.

The fate of the entire airline rested in their hands. Management held its breath.

I thought it was both ironic and appropriate that this multibillion-dollar enterprise's fate lay in the hands of the mostly women who had been perceived in the past as being servants of the customers. How far we had come from the days when the unofficial slogan of the airline was "coffee, tea, or me?"

Today, it seemed to be "coffee, tea, or bankruptcy?" So, I waited like the others to see what the flight attendants would do.

They decided to go along with the other front line workers and make huge concessions in their pay, their hours, and their benefits in order to keep their airline from plunging into bankruptcy.

All was going well until it slipped out that the executives had failed to mention one small detail of the concessions plan. This little, bitty fact was that while everyone else in the airline was taking huge pay cuts, the executives were going to get huge bonuses—equal to double their salaries—as a "thank you" for staying on board. They also were going to get lots of money poured into a guaranteed new pension fund set up especially for them . . . not the same pension fund that was being slashed by the new plan for all the other workers.

There was a huge uproar from the unions. They rightfully felt that they had been betrayed and duped. When the CEO was interviewed, he said in a rather bewildered way, "I thought they would be glad that we were being so aggressive about keeping good talent at the top." Not so.

Boom went the house of cards, and the very CEO who was riding high one day was asked to resign the very next day. The fickle blade of the business guillotine fell not on the necks of the willing sacrificial lambs, but on the CEO himself. Lightbulbs flashed around him as he exited the stage, shocked at what had happened to his status in twenty-four hours. What a difference a day makes.

This official failed to realize that he did not have the right to lord it over the others—as if he and his fellow executives were kings and dukes immune from hunger while the peasants agreed to eat potatoes. All the king's horses and all the king's men couldn't put this CEO together again. The ignorance of pride once again took its toll.

The sad part of the story was that this CEO seems to have been a fairly good man—leading the airline during some of its most profitable and heady days. Unfortunately he took his title of CEO to mean not "Conservator of Excellent Oversight" but "Conqueror Emeritus of Others."

When Joan of Arc was granted any request she wanted upon helping the Dauphin ascend his rightful throne, she asked for only two things. One request: "Please pay off the debt of my uncle and friend who borrowed money to buy me my horse."

"Done!" said the exuberant king. "What else?"

"Don't tax the people of my village for the next four hundred years."

"OK," said the king, gulping this time.

Her requests were honored. This leader thought not of herself, but of her people. She did not lord it over others.

Jesus, knowing that he was God and that he was about to go to God, knelt and washed his disciples' feet. Unlike all too many executives and CEOs who send their people out first to the slaughter, Jesus went forward to meet his executioners, telling them to let the people go and take only him.

Jesus, Lord of lords, saw himself first and foremost as a servant.

Great leaders do the same.

QUESTIONS

1. Where do you use your power to make sure that you avoid suffering, unmindful of what others are going through?

2. What might the CEO of the airline have done instead to make the airline, and his relationships with the unions, more successful?

3. Where in your life has pride caused you to fall?

4. Where is pride lurking in your life now, sticking its foot out with a hidden smile?

Dear Lord,
What a hard lesson. For me. For all of us. King of the mountain is a slippery place. Help me take the lowest place, and in so doing, honor you. Amen.

KNOW THE DIFFERENCE
BETWEEN ARCHETYPE
AND STEREOTYPE

DO NOT KEEP JUDGING ACCORDING TO
APPEARANCES; LET YOUR JUDGEMENT
BE ACCORDING TO WHAT IS RIGHT.
—JOHN 7:24 (NJB)

Nearly 80 percent of new product offerings fail—despite the fact that research showed that customers wanted it, needed it, and would buy it. In the book *How Customers Think*, Harvard researcher Gerald Zaltman argues that 95 percent of thinking happens in the unconscious: "Therefore, unearthing your customer's desires requires you to understand the consumer's hidden mind." Zaltman includes research from diverse disciplines ranging from neurology, sociology, literary analysis, and cognitive science to prove that we must mine the unconscious to determine what we really believe.

He states the difference between archetype and stereotype. An *archetype*, for example, is a character that revolves around a universal theme, such as a journey or challenge—perhaps of a hero trying to find his way home—while a *stereotype* offers a one-dimensional view of a character in a setting, such as a woman doing the dishes. Zaltman argues that in order for marketers to build their brands, they must tap into the universal understanding of archetypal journeys and not settle for stereotypes.

Jesus was a master at delving into the unconscious "journeys" that his followers were on. When he offered the fishermen a chance to become "fishers of men," he was changing them from stereotypes of simple working stiffs to archetypes—embarking on a life-changing and, at times, life-threatening journey.

I am convinced that one of the greatest challenges facing society today is the tendency to stereotype others and thus miss the depth of the journeys that they are on.

The mind sorts in terms of stereotypes. The heart deals in archetypes. And that is where wisdom is to be found.

I was sitting with a friend in Washington, D.C., as we

watched people go by. She pointed out a man who seemed a bit disheveled in his appearance. She said, "That man reminds me of someone who could be a mass murderer."

I said, "Why—because his clothes aren't the best?"

"No," she said, "because he just helped that lady up on the bus so nicely." When I asked her what she meant by her seemingly contradictory statement, she said, "Mass murderers often are no different from you or me. They just have stronger weaknesses."

Jesus was able to look at the prostitute and see her not as the stereotype she seemed. He saw her as a woman who was about to embark on an epic journey into the depths of her soul, through forgiveness, recognition, and repentance.

I am somewhat guilty of judging according to stereotypes and missing the bigger picture. Part of my work at the women's resource center involved counseling battered women and connecting them with resources in the community. I experienced the horror of watching women come in with bruises on their legs the first visit, only to return home and come back to the center in far worse shape.

One woman in particular that I counseled insisted that her husband had repented and wept crocodile tears when he saw the size of the bruise his fist had left on her. My counterparts and I tried to convince her to seek shelter because statistics show that without major intervention, battering only progresses, sometimes even to death. She would hear none of our arguments, however. Two months later she returned in worse shape than before. Her husband had gone into a rage and shattered her jaw. We wept with her as we made arrangements to take her to a safer place.

After three years of beholding such sights, one day I boldly pronounced that no man who ever hit a woman would be welcome in my life. Imagine my surprise when the following holiday I was confronted with exactly that scenario. A coworker I'd befriended shared with me that he was a former wife abuser. He had been arrested six times.

Stereotype: worthless wife beater. Knee-jerk solution: reject him. Which I was prepared to do.

But this phrase kept haunting me, even more than my bold pronouncement: What would Jesus do? How had Jesus looked at my coworker when he emerged from jail? He had served his time, expressed his deep remorse, and was now attending anger management classes. And the only terms I could think of were *unconditional positive regard*. So, I determined to look at him with unconditional positive regard and reject my natural inclination (which was along the lines of desiring someone to hire some street thugs to beat him up so he could see what it felt like to be beaten black and blue).

A couple of weeks after he told me about his past, he and I sat down at a Burger King. We chewed our food, sipped our sodas, and didn't quite know what to say to each other. I was in no position to judge him, or influence him, really. He didn't work for me, he wasn't related to me, and our worlds were very different. He had just gotten a promotion, and I asked him how that was going. He began to talk about it, and then one thing led to another, and suddenly I was hearing how his mother had abused him both verbally and physically, as had his father. What unfolded was a tale of a childhood that was more than difficult—it was tragic.

Yet to his credit, this man was determined to see that his young daughter knew her father, and that her father was present in her life, despite the temptations to go back to his old, violent habits.

Suddenly I realized that he was on his own epic journey.

He looked down at his little girl laughing in the playground nearby, and said, "This has been the hardest year of my life. But I am not going to give up." He sighed, pointing to his daughter, and added, "I only have fifteen more years to go before she leaves home." This man was more than the stereotype he appeared to be. He was embarking on the archetypal journey of becoming a good father when he had no positive role models.

I ended up asking him how I could help him and encouraged him to attend his court-appointed anger management classes, which I knew were just the beginning of deep therapy work he needed. He thanked me for listening to him and then called for his daughter to go home.

Was anything solved or made better that day? Only my own understanding. I kept thinking about the blind man who received his first touch from Jesus. Whereas before he could see nothing, he now said, "I see men as trees walking." He required yet a second touch from Jesus before he could see people clearly. Perhaps you and I are like that—requiring a second touch from the hand of God before we see people not as frozen stereotypes to be judged, but as emerging archetypes, potential heroes who are finding their way home.

Stereotype or archetype? Jesus knew the difference. He calls us to as well.

QUESTIONS

1. Which groups of people most anger you? List as many of them as you can.

2. Why do they make you angry?

3. Can you view each of them as a hidden hero on a secret journey to his or her own redemption, saved by the grace of God?

4. Who might see you as a stereotype?

5. How wrong would they be?

6. Define your own epic journey, realizing that you are not alone.

Dear Lord,

Help me not see people as one dimensional, easily labeled, and thus dismissed stereotypes, but as the potential heroes they are. Help me view them with unconditional positive regard, just as you view me.

Thank you for your amazing grace. Amen and Amen.

LEARN A NEW WAY

OF DUSTING

BUT WHATEVER CITY YOU ENTER, AND THEY DO
NOT RECEIVE YOU, GO OUT INTO ITS STREETS
AND SAY, "THE VERY DUST OF YOUR CITY WHICH
CLINGS TO US WE WIPE OFF AGAINST YOU."
—LUKE 10:10–11 (NKJV)

Fill in the blank in the following sentence (it is from the Bible):

"Suddenly the whole city set out to meet Jesus; and as soon as they saw him they _____."

Here are your choices:

(a)   asked him to heal the sick among them
(b)   asked him to feed their hungry
(c)   asked him to teach them about God
(d)   asked him to leave their neighborhood

The answer is *d*. They actually "implored" him to leave their neighborhood (Matt. 8:34 NJB). Jesus, Coach, was upsetting so many people in the town that they asked him to leave.

Don't think for a moment that when you are suddenly clear about your mission and vision and you head out to do miracles, you are always going to be welcomed by others. In fact, Jesus made it perfectly clear that people who were full of his Spirit were going to be rejected and, like him, asked to leave.

Going back to the example, what did Jesus do in this instance? Did he dig in and work harder to try to win these people's approval? Did he call down fire and thunder, barbecuing the lot of them? Or did he simply, quietly, and respectfully leave? Quite simply, he left.

Jesus never stayed in a place where he wasn't welcome. Nor did he force his gifts on anyone who didn't want them. It showed the ultimate respect of God for people's free will, even when it is misinformed. Leaving people alone in this misery was perhaps the hardest thing Jesus had had to do. But he did it. And so can you.

There is something quiveringly pure about Christ, and it is this: he never sold off pieces of himself to the highest bidder. Take me, or leave me, he said. But be willing to face me.

One only has to listen to the radio to hear a small portion of the many unhealthy, unhappy, and off-center relationships in this world. I don't know what it is about us that makes us willing to bend ourselves into unrecognizable shapes trying to get others' approval, but we do. Too many of us aren't people; we're pretzels—trying to please every person who has ever laid eyes on us.

Jesus said this to his disciples: "Go and tell them what you've personally seen and heard—how the lame walk, the deaf hear, and the blind now see. And if they do not receive you, do this—dust off your shoes, and go on to the next town."

He *didn't* say, "Camp out and howl on their doorstop. Whine underneath their windows, hoping they'll see you." He said. "Just simply show some self-respect and leave."

Why don't we leave situations when it is clear that our spirits are not being received? I think the main reason we stay is that we're afraid. But if Jesus is your Coach, you will not allow the dust of fear and neglect to settle around you. He wants you in an atmosphere of open, eager, willing listeners—people who will believe in you, just as his friends believed in him.

Having Jesus as your Coach may cause a few doors to be slammed in your face, but if you are willing to dust off those shoes and keep moving, your feet will be dancing soon enough.

QUESTIONS

1. Where are you currently not being received?

2. Is it at work? At home? In your family?

3. How much dust is in your house—the house of your inner life?

Dear Lord,
Let's get out some dust cloths today. Help me see my way clear to lead a dust-free existence, surrounded by people who receive me fresh every morning, just as you do. Amen.

KNOW THAT HE
IS DRIVEN BY A DESIRE
TO SEE YOU SUCCEED

[LOVE] BEARS ALL THINGS, BELIEVES ALL
THINGS, HOPES ALL THINGS.
—1 CORINTHIANS 13:7 (NRSV)

Many of the financially successful women I have known had fathers who were adamant about seeing them succeed. My father had high hopes of my being a professional tennis player. He was convinced that I could succeed in that sport, and he invested a lot of time and energy in trying to get me there. However, I chose another path.

I will never forget how much he wanted me to win—to be the best at something. Right before one of my major sports tournaments I asked Mom where Dad was. She said, "He doesn't want me to tell you this, honey, but he's in the bathroom throwing up. I think he's even more excited and nervous about your match than you are."

Two aspects of successful coaching include setting high standards and being passionately interested in seeing your client win. Jesus demonstrated both qualities.

He had such a passionate desire to see all living creatures lifted up that he even grieved when he saw a baby bird that had fallen from its nest and thus would never fly. He walked around his world seeing and seeking those who could be better, do better, live more fully. He noticed the man with the withered hand, and he joined his belief to the man's belief that indeed it could be well. He noticed the invalid by the pool of Bethesda, who had somehow been overlooked for thirty-eight years. Jesus spoke only a few words to that man, and that man got off his mat and walked (John 5:5–9).

When he said, "I came that they may have life, and have it abundantly" (John 10:10 NRSV), he was talking about you and me—he was talking to you and me. His entire being, his total focus, his entire life, was about seeing you and me succeed.

I am reminded of a woman who admitted to me that she had to be restrained during high school football games because whenever her son caught the ball, she jumped out of her chair and actually ran alongside him on the field. There is a book titled *Are You Running with Me, Jesus?* And the answer is yes, yes, and always yes. No matter what the score.

Wherever you are, whatever your circumstances, you must know that Jesus desperately wants to be your Coach, and he is motivated by nothing more than seeing you succeed, in every sense of the word.

QUESTIONS

1. Have you ever had someone in your life who was passionate about seeing you succeed? Who was that person, and how did it make you feel? If you didn't, how did that affect you?

2. Do you believe that individual saw you, or was he or she only trying to live vicariously?

3. Can you visualize Jesus as your Coach today, looking at you and seeing unending possibilities?

4. Can you see him beside you even now, asking how you want your life to be better?

Dear Lord,
You came to earth so that I and anyone who heard your voice could respond and win at this game called life. Help me to

receive and believe the fact that your goal and heart's desire is only for my good, and then help me listen and respond to your leadings. Amen.

BE BATHED
IN LOVING WORDS

HOW BEAUTIFUL YOU ARE, MY BELOVED,
HOW BEAUTIFUL YOU ARE!
—SONG OF SONGS 4:1 (NJB)

I wince whenever I encounter couples whose behavior toward each other in public is that of the Bickersons. One of them says something, and the other corrects whatever was said. One of them starts to tell a joke, and the other steals the punch line. Some couples feel that wherever two or more or gathered, it's time to get out the boxing gloves and duke it out in front of an audience. Insults and put-downs start flying, and those around them have to duck or be caught in the crossfire.

After one such very long evening, I got into a discussion with a friend who had also witnessed the "discussion." I said, "That is so sad." To me, the purpose of a relationship is to lift each other up . . . to honor and cherish and revere the other . . . not hold the other underwater until the person yells, "I give up. You win!"

My friend shook his head and agreed. "There are two types of relationships in the world—those who take lovers, and those who take hostages. Evidently the couple we were with were in a voluntary hostage situation."

Not too long ago the nation was stunned by the videotape from a surveillance camera that recorded a mother pummeling her young daughter in a parking lot. The tape showed the mother looking to her right and left as she loaded the daughter in the backseat, as if to make sure no one was around to notice, and then she began to beat the little girl unmercifully while the child was strapped into the car seat!

Statistics show that such violent behavior is rampant in our society. It just so happened that this singular incident was caught on tape. In my hometown of El Paso, Texas, last year nine thousand children were removed from their homes and taken into protective custody. Not nine. Not ninety or even nine hundred. Nine *thousand* children. And that was only in one city, and that figure reflected only those cases that were bad enough, visible enough, flagrant enough, to get reported. This is an outrage.

Should a mother beat her child? No.

Should a husband beat his wife? No.

Should a teacher beat up a student? No.

Should a coach beat up an athlete? No.

Should a God beat up his creation? Oops . . . if you started to say an automatic no there, are you really so sure about that? Or do you have an image of a God who is always mad at you . . . always grading or scolding you . . . always waiting to catch you doing something wrong . . . always mad at you for something? Unfortunately this is the image of God that much of religion teaches today.

I visit different denominations when I go to new cities, and last Sunday I went to one that had a very big building and a very big parking lot. I sat there with great expectation and hope and was eventually sorry that I entered the door of the sanctuary. The preacher stood and began to literally yell at us about how we should be doing things. I left to go to the restroom and was alarmed to find the children with solemn faces, high-step marching in a perfect line from one room to another.

If Jesus came to tell us anything, it is that ours is not an angry Father. God is not waiting with stick in hand raised to punish us; he is the eager Father, watching and waiting every day for us to come home. And when we do, what will he do? Throw a party to celebrate our return . . . to celebrate his love for *us*.

Before you can accept that Jesus wants to affirm you,

you need to accept the foundational basis of a God who loves you. Not many of us can do that.

When you enter into a coaching relationship with Jesus, you will be surprised at how affirming he really is. He will lovingly notice your strengths and encourage you in them. He will cover you with blessings and joy and celebration, and thus bring your performance to a new level of divine excellence. Affirmation is the nature of your Coach. Get ready to accept it.

QUESTIONS

1. Are you in relationships that are affirming or degrading?

2. Do you fear God, thinking that you will be punished if you enter into a closer relationship?

3. How do you beat *yourself* up when no one else is watching?

Dear Lord,
You created me in love. Help me believe and receive your loving words to me. Help me rise with you into all I can be. Help me see myself in your eyes. Amen and amen.

PRODUCTIVITY

Scripture gives us beautiful passages about how important productivity and fruitfulness are to both God and humans. The first commandment we receive in the book of Genesis is "to be fruitful and multiply." The prophet Ezekiel offers us a beautiful image of a river that gets deeper and wider: "Along the bank of the river, on this side and that, will grow all kinds of trees used for food; their leaves will not wither, and their fruit will not fail. They will bear fruit every month, because their water flows from the sanctuary. Their fruit will be for food, and their leaves for medicine" (Ezek. 47:12 NKJV). Jesus said that those who abide in him, and sink their roots deep into his love and his being, would be fruitful.

All our busyness often masks a misconception of what it means to be productive. Productivity isn't about doing more and more or even about accomplishment. Does a tree "accomplish" bearing fruit? Or is the fruit merely a manifestation of what was inside the tree all along? Fruit also comes in due time, looks different in different stages, and is good to behold and to eat. Are your deeds—those that are produced by your busyness—the same?

In this section we'll look at how Jesus can help you increase your productivity—mostly through "being."

COME ALIVE
WITH NEW
POSSIBILITIES

YES, I KNOW WHAT PLANS I HAVE
IN MIND FOR YOU.
—JEREMIAH 29:11 (NJB)

As I was flying to New York recently for a private party held in my honor, I marveled at the turn my life had taken. Just a few years ago I was a stressed-out advertising agency executive, dealing with personnel problems on my staff and worrying about the mounting overhead costs caused by my goals of expansion. I remember so clearly days when I dreaded getting out of bed. Now I can scarcely receive the good that flows all around me. And I can attribute the turn-around in my life to a simple three-letter word. "Yes." When I was able to finally face and confront my lingering passion concerning Jesus as a business leader, I said, "Yes," to a huge unknown, and I have been blessed beyond imagining ever since. "Yes" opened the door to new possibilities.

On the layover in the Dallas–Fort Worth airport, I picked up a copy of *USA Today* and was fascinated by an article titled "New Findings Throw Physicists for a Loop." The article stated that while physicists have long felt that protons, the positively charged elements within an atom, are shaped like balls, it turns out that they are actually ellip-tical in shape. People in a lab who were intrigued by this were able to determine that protons are elliptical because the quarks bubbling up inside them are actually comprised of smaller elements that *are moving at the speed of light.*

I related this new information to findings of several years ago that there are tiny particles which seem to respond to the expectation of their observers, despite the fact that their essence is identical. In other words, if scien-tists in England expected these particles to behave a certain way, they did, while scientists in Australia might come up with different behaviors for the very same element based on what *they* expected to find

Sometimes I picture Jesus as a trapeze artist, dangling from a moving swing, reaching out to me eagerly, calling me to leave my comfort zone. If I choose to make the leap, he will catch me. If I choose to stay where I am, I cannot then honestly say, "God didn't answer my prayer for a better life."

Yet I hear people say that all the time. And when I hear that, I wonder if Jesus is still dangling and swinging patiently, waiting for them to *believe* he will catch them when they let go of the trapeze they are clinging to.

Life with Jesus is a dance of possibilities far more than the march of sorrows we have come to associate with religion. I walked the Via Dolorosa several years ago and will never forget it. I touched the walls on the path where the guards pulled Simon the Cyrene out to help Jesus carry his cross. I stared at the tomb where legend and archaeological experts estimate that he lay, and I was moved to tears.

But I never forget that we—you and I—turned the music off and made him die on a cross. His life was about turning water into wine, and dancing with people who used to be lame and placing on their heads a garland made of flowers taken from lilies in the field. He said, "Wipe off the dust from your feet." Don't hang around negative people. Don't believe the lies that you are worthless or unimportant. Don't buy for a minute the illusion that your money will comfort you more than the relationship you can have with me. Shift your orientation away from sorrow and pain and toward the light of laughter and dance and joy.

Follow me, and I will take you places you never even knew existed.

Follow me, and I will cause you to leap like deer in the dawn.

Follow me, and we will climb mountains and get through valleys and come out of them on top, laughing, living, holding each other, into eternity.

This is the Jesus, the Coach, that I know. What do you say to him most—yes or no?

QUESTIONS

1. Is your life more like a funeral dirge than a dance right now? Why might that be?

2. Would you be willing to lift up your eyes to the hills, or do you prefer to keep them turned down to the valley?

3. When was the last time you took a risk in the direction of your dance?

4. How comfortable can you be, for how long, hanging upside down on your trapeze anyway?

Dear Lord,
You are the Lord of the dance, of life, of all possibilities. Help me turn my eyes toward you and see in them all that I can be, can do, can learn, can live, in this relationship with you. Amen.

UNDERSTAND

RELATIONSHIP

ECONOMIES

"YOU SHALL LOVE THE LORD . . . [AND]
LOVE YOUR NEIGHBOR AS YOURSELF." ON
THESE TWO COMMANDMENTS HANG
ALL THE LAW AND THE PROPHETS.
—MATTHEW 22:37–40 (NRSV)

My friend Bonnie is a smiling Southern gal who, due to her training as a family systems therapist, can deliver a punch of truth to the gut and smile while she's doing so. Her specialty is getting to the heart of things quickly, without apology, and having you end up saying thank you after the surgery. One day at an after-dinner gathering of women, she said, "I tell teenagers and parents, poor people and billionaires the same thing. When you die, you take only two things with you—memories and relationships. So you'd best start developing them now."

Imagine if your life focus became that—developing and treasuring happy memories and fulfilling relationships. How wealthy would you be?

Studies show you'd be healthier, for one thing. Just this morning I was reading an article in the *Arizona Republic* stating that a study revealed that elderly people who reached out and helped others lived longer and healthier lives than those who dwelt only on themselves. Somehow endorphins are released when people give. Psychologists who conducted the study called it "The Helpers' High."

I remember feeling a wave of goodwill wash over me one day as I was involved in a gathering of adults who had assembled from long distances for only one purpose—to determine what kind of help the four-year-old girl needed to go from someone who could not form words properly to someone who could speak clearly. In all the meetings in which I have been a participant, most of which deal with strategies for business development or the growth of companies, I never quite felt this kind of "goodwill wave" wash over me. All the talent and technology in the room was focused on one budding human being: Just how could we help her talk and walk and smile?

The mother was interviewed, reports were generated, action plans delineated, and the little girl just rested her head on her mother's shoulder, unaware that all this activity was dedicated to helping her have a normal life.

A friend of mine who sold his company for many millions of dollars became aware that his life was going to shift suddenly from "earning money" to "having money." When he conducted an impromptu study of other multimillionaires who had sold their companies recently, he discovered that nearly 75 percent of them were divorced within a year. This finding gives rise to speculation about the cause. One friend wondered about the men in that group, "Were the wives just hanging in there until the money came in? Were the husbands so lacking in relationship skills that when they finally had spare time to give to the family, there was no family left?"

A classic case of being money-minded more than relationship-minded was given to me the other day. Another dear friend of mine, whom I shall call Bill, had used a unique style of time-honored friendliness to help build up $10 million of business for a company that had recently gone public. The new CEO, "Jim," who was an accountant by trade, began to berate Bill for his expense account, his bills for flowers sent to secretaries and other gatekeepers, his habit of dropping by to see people when there was no official "business reason." Bill got so tired of being nickel-and-dimed by Jim, who spent more time on his expense report than on his sales report, Bill decided to quit. When he called the president of the company, who was a longtime friend, to inform him why he was leaving, he said, "I can't operate in a climate like this. It is either going to be Jim or me." The president, "Lou," was unable to commit to Bill that Sam's employment would be terminated, so Bill resigned.

Bill told Jim, "What you don't understand, Jim, is that in times like these, we have what we call a relationship economy. I don't have a noncompete with you or this company, and I guarantee that 90 percent of those clients are going to walk out the door with me." And they did.

Lou, realizing the hemorrhage that was about to occur, went to the chairman of the holding company and pleaded his case. Ten days later Bill was offered his old job back, at more money, and Jim, the penny-pinching CEO, had been escorted out of the building. Sam was straining at gnats and missing the camels, and Bill knew it.

I loved when he used those words *relationship economy* because that is surely what we are in. When times get hard economically it is only the web and wealth of our relationships that carry us through.

Several years ago we watched CEOs of some of the world's largest corporations get led away in handcuffs because of their deceitfulness about the financial condition of their companies. Their downfall caused the loss of over $3 trillion—causing many well-meaning people to lose their retirement funds. Where did all that money go? Much of it went into the pockets of people who had no real accountability in their relationships with others.

Author Matthew Fox offers a challenging, Orwellian thesis in his book *Sins of the Spirit*. He states that since corporations are legal entities that can live perpetually, it is conceivable that eventually these nameless, faceless, unaccountable entities could use nameless, faceless technologies to bring us humans, and the planet, to our collective knees. When there is no real face behind a decision, who is to blame?

Hitler was able to incorporate a mass generational madness of economic, ecological, and spiritual disaster when he began teaching that Jews were not really people, but an inferior species. By rendering them less than "relational," he made them easier to obliterate.

When Jesus said, "When you did it to one of the least of these my brothers and sisters, you were doing it to me!" (Matt. 25:40 NLT), he was saying that every person is worthy of the same respect *you would give to God*. Do we practice this in everyday life? Do you? Do I?

Undergirding every principle that Jesus taught is the importance of your relationship to God, to others, and to yourself. He said it was the sum of all wisdom, all law, all prophets. Yet daily we trample over people to get to money, power, fame, or glory. Jesus said, "What does it profit you if you gain the whole world and lose your own soul?" (my paraphrase of Mark 8:36). If ever there were a way that the soul would be defined, it would have to be in terms of its relationships.

How is your soul doing these days?

Jesus wants to know.

QUESTIONS

1. What do you think is meant by the term *relationship economy?*

2. If your stock portfolio fell into the minus-zero range, who or what would determine your wealth?

3. What groups of people have you, consciously or unconsciously, decided are not worthy of being "related to"?

4. Which groups did Jesus say were so?

Dear Lord,

Help me remember that in your world, relationships are not everything; they are the only thing. Help me remember that my net worth is determined by my heart's work, especially with others, in your name. Amen.

NOT RECEIVE

BORROWED ARMOR

SAUL DRESSED DAVID IN HIS OWN ARMOUR; HE
PUT A BRONZE HELMET ON HIS HEAD, DRESSED
HIM IN A BREASTPLATE AND BUCKLED HIS OWN
SWORD OVER DAVID'S ARMOUR. DAVID TRIED TO
WALK BUT, NOT BEING USED TO THEM, SAID TO
SAUL, "I CANNOT WALK IN THESE; I AM NOT
USED TO THEM." SO THEY TOOK THEM OFF AGAIN.
1 SAMUEL 17:38–39 (NJB)

As the crowd gathered in the magnificent ballroom, the
young man named Miko began in earnest to tell the stories of

Homer's *Iliad* and *Odyssey*—sharing how the mythic journeys in these epics had helped him find his own place and point of power in corporate America. He shared that in one scene two men were meeting: one, a great warrior, was burned out and disgusted by the low pay and nonexistent praise he had been receiving from management (sound familiar?); the other, a relative newcomer, was desperate to prove himself on the field of battle. The younger one said to the older, "I have a great idea! Let me borrow your armor. Then people will perceive me as you and run in terror." The disheartened worker took off his armor and gave it to the young man, who then proceeded to wear it confidently into battle. To make a long story short—the man in the borrowed armor was soundly beaten and humiliated, literally chased off the field. It seems the borrowed armor fooled no one but himself.

This concept of borrowed armor did not originate with the Greeks. In fact, Adam used it when he tried to convince God that it was actually his wife, Eve, who made him eat that apple. Eve said she wasn't responsible; it was the serpent that made her indulge. In the Genesis story God was not fooled—he knew exactly who said and did what, regardless of what they were trying to hide behind.

King Saul tried to give young David his armor—convinced that the young shepherd boy didn't have a chance against Goliath going it on his own. David allowed them to fit him with someone else's armor—the king's. Yet within minutes he knew that it wasn't him, and he shed it in order to be himself, depending solely on his relationship with God.

In my book *Teach Your Team to Fish: Using Ancient Wisdom for Visionary Teamwork*, I have a chapter titled "He Taught There Was No Them." In it I make the point that Jesus kept bringing responsibility for success or failure squarely back to the individual—never allowing the excuse of a "them" to be used for failure. As I traveled the country on the tour promoting the book, I shared this chapter frequently, and each time people began nodding and poking one another. It seems the concept of "them" is alive and well in organizations and teams everywhere. "We can't do this because of them . . . If only they hadn't done x, we could do y." Those excuses do not fly in heaven.

Another side of the "them" excuse is trying to hide inside someone else's armor—seeking to use the other's reputation or strength or money to buy prestige and honor. When someone steals another's idea and claims it as his own, that is using borrowed armor. When a husband thinks his wife's virtue is going to get him into heaven, that is using borrowed armor. When a wife expects her husband to handle all financial affairs, that is using borrowed armor. When we allow others to speak or act for us, that is using borrowed armor.

A friend has the political skills and popularity to easily win election in his city. A good ol' boy farmer, he is savvy when it comes to affairs of state. When I asked him one time why he didn't run for office, he smiled and said, "I learned from my daddy that it is better to own a politician than be one." We both laughed at his remark.

Yet it occurred to me the other day that when we elect others to represent us, we are actually letting them borrow *our* armor. They are supposed to speak for us and act like us and spend our money on our behalf. How successful is that?

A common topic in my speeches is the trap and fallacy of parallel careers—how people settle for being close to doing what they love rather than actually doing it. A person who works in a frame shop to be around artists, but is actually afraid to paint, is living in borrowed armor. An advertising executive who really longs to write novels, but makes a living writing for other people, is living in borrowed armor.

Jesus doesn't allow for that. In fact, he will look right through whatever outfit you are wearing and get right to the truth of things.

An example was the woman at the well, who tried to engage him in distracting dialogue about philosophy rather than let him see into her soul. He looked right through her pretend game and told her to realize that he knew what she had been up to, and it was time to draw water for herself.

We are living in borrowed armor when we allow others to entertain and engage and live for us—whether it is through the media or our children.

A friend sent me a cartoon that showed a Little League coach talking to a bunch of children. He said, "Okay, kids, now go out there and have fun. Remember, your parents are living vicariously through you." Parents who live through their children are living in borrowed armor.

Jesus said that the yoke he fashioned for you would be easy, and the burden would be light. That is because he is a custom tailor, if you will, and does not desire or accept that you wear someone else's clothes.

You need no other armor but what he provides for you. He will not give you borrowed armor. And it will be tailor made.

QUESTIONS

1. Where in your life are you living through someone else—either in blame or in longing?

2. What might it feel like to actually walk in your own set of armor?

3. If you examine the failures of your past, how many of them might be attributed to the fact that you were wearing borrowed armor?

Dear Lord,
Help me realize that you are my Cloak and my Shield. I need no other armor than the truth of your love. Amen.

NOT BE

"CHILDIZED"

WHEN I WAS A CHILD, I USED TO . . . THINK LIKE
A CHILD; BUT NOW THAT I HAVE BECOME AN
ADULT, I HAVE FINISHED WITH ALL CHILDISH WAYS.
—1 CORINTHIANS 13:11 (NJB)

It has been one of my privileges in life to befriend numerous social workers and therapists. (This has no doubt saved me a lot of money as well because I get the benefit of their wisdom over lunches rather than on $125-an-hour couches.) One of these friends is a counselor who suffered many abandonment issues from his childhood and entered therapy himself as a young man to try to remediate his unhappy past. After several years of therapy he developed an incredibly supportive and close relationship with his therapist, only to hit a financial snag that prevented him from being able to continue with the meetings. When he approached his therapist about the possibility of being able to continue the therapy as a friend at a much-reduced rate, his therapist responded with this sentence and her own made-up word: "I refuse to 'childize' you. Therefore, I will continue to treat you as an adult who must pay for professional services at standard fees."

When Robert told me this, I asked him to repeat the word *"childize"* because I had never heard it before. When I asked for an explanation, he said that it means that a person sees another no longer as an adult, but as a child, and begins to treat that person as such. Obviously his therapist didn't want to do that. Robert said that as angry and hurt as that statement made him at the time, he sees it as a "breaking through" point in his life: "It made me realize that I really was an adult and should start behaving as one in every area. I had continued to see myself as an 'abandoned child' in many ways, and the area of finances was one of them. When I ran out of money, I expected this person to 'take care of me.' She didn't, and from that point on I began to stop seeing myself as being a helpless child in every way."

Dietrich Bonhoeffer was a Lutheran theologian during

World War Two who began to question the social policies and politics of his time—becoming adamantly opposed to the rise of Nazism in his native country. He was ultimately executed for his involvement in a plot to assassinate Hitler. His *Letters and Papers from Prison*, written in the two years before his execution, is ranked as one of the top ten spiritual books of the twentieth century.

In one these letters Bonhoeffer wrote, "Religious people speak of God when human perception and human resources fail . . . *(this is often just from laziness.)*" He went on to say that until humanity begins to take up the grail of social responsibility and mature actions in light of a sense of compassionate community, we are only mouthing words that in effect make God a machine—Something that comes to our aid when we have stopped trying to solve problems of our own making.

Jesus taught accountability and participation in life. When he said, "Follow me, and I will make you fishers of human souls," he was talking about expanded being and thinking—not as a child looking for its next mouthful, but as an adult seeking to shape the world.

As my friend Jackie Brewton says so eloquently, "We live beneath our Divine Privilege." With that privilege comes responsibility.

Yet I am often guilty of asking God merely for things . . . for success . . . for protection . . . for safety for myself and my loved ones . . . for a painless life and an ease-filled passing into an even better place. When I do that, am I a Christian, or merely a mouthy papoose, strapped on to God for dear life, wanting only to be fed and cared for?

When you accept Jesus as your Life Coach, be aware of what you are asking for. It may not involve physical suffering. Very few people in the free world die martyrs' deaths anymore. But it will involve the tearing down of your self-imposed boundaries and limitations. He will demolish your comfort zone and ask you to take on more responsibility than you ever knew was possible. Not necessarily responsibility for someone else, but for yourself—your soul—your own eternal beingness.

Jesus knows what you are capable of far more than you do. He did not show up at this point in your life just to take you to the zoo. My friend Amy said that when she encountered Christ, it was like walking into a fun house at the circus: "The entrance seemed okay at first, but suddenly nothing seemed to be on even ground anymore."

Jesus will rock your world. And you will begin, as an adult, to learn what it is to be mature in an uncertain, uneven, unfair world, where you and I are called to be the eyes and arms and ears of Christ . . . taking up our part in the true Christian community of compassion and social action rather than riding on a playground of carousels pushed by leaders with their own agendas.

QUESTIONS

1. Where in your life are you still acting like a child?

2. How do you think God views that?

3. When does "faith" really begin to look like childlike begging?

4. What is the difference?

Dear Lord,
Help me become a Christian who keeps you company rather than one who requires a pacifier and diaper bag. Amen.

PRACTICE POSITIVE

CONFRONTATION

IF YOUR BROTHER DOES SOMETHING WRONG,
REBUKE HIM AND, IF HE IS SORRY, FORGIVE HIM.
—LUKE 17:3 (NJB)

I was watching a television report on the new automobile show held every year in Detroit where they feature the hottest "rods" coming down the road. The reporter was focusing on car colors and a psychological study that was supposed to reveal a person's personality by the color of the car he or she drives. Apparently white is the most commonly selected car color in America, and it signifies "a desire to blend in." That did not strike me as being a particularly good thing.

In an adult church discussion group I attended last Sunday, questions were raised about the relevancy of the church and Christianity in America today. The facilitator asked, "How much of religion is culture?" And the group took off on that. He made the point that every experience you or I have is mediated by and interpreted through the filter of our culture. If that is true, a culture that decides cars that blend in will sell better than cars that don't is helping teach us subconsciously and pervasively that it is not a good thing to stand out.

Images of Nazi Germany and Stepford "look-alike" wives begin to march through my head when I contemplate how many of us are afraid to take an unpopular stand or engage in positive confrontation.

In a bone-chilling tour I took with my friend Linda through the museum of the concentration camp in Mauthausen, Austria, we learned that Hitler began as a best-selling author who then infiltrated the education system with false scientific reports about the superiority of the German race. Students were taught that it was not okay to confront authorities or ask questions of any kind of their teachers. They were taught how to dress and act and what roles each should play, and within a matter of decades Hitler had himself a culture of compliance—one that was easy to manipulate into a devastating war.

This cultural overhang was poignantly brought home to me when I spoke in Vienna about entrepreneurism. The hall was packed to capacity with Austrians who were curious about this blend of spirituality and business that I had written about in my first book *Jesus, CEO*. After I exhorted the attendees to find their unique mission in life, and then go do it, a number of people approached me afterward. The one question on their lips was this: "Where do we go to ask permission to do this?"

"To do what?" I asked.

"To start a business of our own."

I was looking into the faces of a one-generation-removed audience—people in their thirties and forties—whose parents had been taught on pain of death that you do not stand out or strike out on your own.

Jesus was a master at the art of positive confrontation. It is only when you and I are willing to ask the hard questions, first of ourselves and then of others, that we will begin to move into the higher levels of true prosperity and fulfillment.

In his award-winning movie *Bowling for Columbine*, Michael Moore films two students who survived the Columbine massacre, yet still had bullets lodged inside them. Upon learning that the bullets used were purchased at a local K-Mart, Moore takes these two kids to the international headquarters of K-Mart and asks to speak to the CEO. A media spokeswoman emerges, informs them that the CEO will not be in for a week, but if they write their questions down, she will see that they get answered.

Moore states, "I brought these students here promising them that they would get a hearing from someone in authority." She goes back upstairs. Two hours later there emerges the man whose job it is to purchase the ammunition sold throughout the stores. The man is understandably nervous and uncomfortable around Moore and the cameras, and he seems distracted as the boys lift their shirts and show the scars from the bullets that went into them. The man turns on his heel and says over his shoulder, "We'll get back to you in a week."

Moore and the boys leave the headquarters in discouragement, feeling that nothing will come from the meeting. Yet two days later there is a press conference where the spokeswoman says, "We are pleased to announce that effective ninety days from today, K-Mart will no longer be selling ammunition for handguns."

Moore and the boys are elated, having never dreamed that their tactics of positive confrontation would actually get them anywhere. The spokeswoman goes on to state that the meeting held between the executives, Michael Moore, and the student survivors of Columbine had affected them deeply and directly led to K-Mart's change in policy.

Time magazine selected as Persons of the Year for 2002 the "whistle-blowers" of Enron, WorldCom, and the FBI—who had openly confronted their superiors about flaws in the system—flaws that proved to be, in every case, fatal. When interviewed by the magazine reporter, each was asked if she felt like a hero. "Oh, no," replied one of them. "I was raised to tell the truth and to stand up for what's right. Isn't that what this country is about?"

Jesus often began his "coaching sessions" with a positive confrontation: "Do you want to be healed? Where is your husband? Who do you think I am?" He did not mince words or always try to be polite when it came to getting to the truth of things. He stated over and over again, "The truth shall set you free."

Unless and until we learn the art of positive confrontation, change will not take place—either in our individual lives or in society. There are conversations that you probably know you need to have, but are afraid to have. What are they?

Jesus will teach you positive confrontation.

QUESTIONS

1. What courageous and positive confrontations do you need to have in your life today?

2. What is the difference between a positive confrontation and an out-and-out attack?

3. Whom can you get as your ally and role player to rehearse this courageous and confrontational conversation?

4. Do you confuse being nice with being true?

Dear Lord,
You know that I need to have some hard talks with a few people. Give me the courage and the follow-through to do so. Amen.

RECEIVE BREAD—
MULTIPLIED

HE TOOK BREAD, GAVE THANKS AND BROKE IT.
—LUKE 22:19 (NKJV)

Jesus, on earth, never created something from nothing.

Jesus used water that was already there in order to make wine. He used a fish's mouth to deliver a coin to pay temple tax. He fed the five thousand by first taking a piece of bread that had been offered to him, giving thanks, breaking it, and then distributing it to the people gathered all around.

When Elijah needed food, he approached a starving widow, who said she had enough crust left to feed only herself and her son. He asked her if she had any oil in the house. She said she was just about out of that, too. (God has a way of meeting people when they are hanging by a thread and then asking them for more rope.) When the trusting widow brought her jar of oil, the oil was miraculously multiplied, leaving her not only enough for her lamp, but also enough to sell and support herself and her son.

Two principles are key here. The first is that *surrender of what you have is always required*. Had the wedding caterers not been willing to bring jars of water, there would have been no wine. Had the little boy not given up his lunch, there would have been no picnic. Had the widow hidden her measly little jar of oil, it would have sputtered out and left her and her son in darkness. So, whatever God is asking you to do, do. Surrender. Give it up. I once wrote a little poem that reads, "When Love comes looking for the Love in you, turn it all over. That's all you can do."

The second principle to remember is that *whatever you offer up is going to change form*. It may look broken and/or smashed to smithereens in the process, but it will be multiplied.

Many of us go to job interviews thinking we need to have all the answers and all the appropriate qualifications. We are trained in our culture to always look good and try— no matter what—to keep it together. The wonderful thing about Jesus is that he looks at what you have, transforms it, and multiplies it in ways you never could have imagined.

Sometimes I picture Jesus sitting in a chair. Someone

comes up and says, "I would like to apply for a job with you." Jesus, like little Bam Bam on *The Flintstones*, reaches out, shakes that person's hand, and proceeds to flip him and trounce him with lightninglike speed, only to leave him standing, looking stunned but nonetheless better, stronger, and happier than before.

The resources you began with will not be recognizable to you when you are through. Their essence might be the same, but they will be multiplied. Whether it is a picnic basket with food left over, when you thought you had enough only for yourself, or a boat that is about to go under with all the fish that are flopping on its deck, you will be amazed at what the Lord will do for you, through you, if you offer him what you have.

Your bread will be multiplied.

QUESTIONS

1. What resource do you have right now that feels inadequate?

2. What will happen if you offer it up, as the little boy did?

Dear Lord,
Take what I have, such as it is, and multiply it according to your will. I am prepared to stand amazed. Amen.

SWIM

UPSTREAM

"CAST THE NET ON THE RIGHT
SIDE OF THE BOAT . . . "
JOHN 21:6 (NKJV)

There is a notion among many Christians that "if God is in this, the doors will swing open." Although that is many times true, sometimes it is not.

The danger of teaching the saying as if it were a hard-and-fast spiritual truth is that sometimes God's will does not take the path of least resistance. Remember, the path of least resistance is often downhill.

For example, Moses had to go to Pharaoh seven times in order for the patriarch to get the message that it was time to let the Israelites go.

What if Moses had made one trip to the palace and declared, "Let my people go," only to have Pharaoh say, "No"? (Which is exactly what happened.) If Moses' coach at that time had believed "if God is in this, the doors will swing open," Moses would have headed back to the desert, only to herd sheep for another forty years.

But Moses learned painfully and painstakingly that when God instructs you to do something, you do it, whether doors swing open or not. "Faith is the substance of things hoped for, the evidence of things not seen" (Heb. 11:1). When God calls you to have faith, it will be when doors seem closed.

Believe me, I have been on both sides of doors—those that swung open naturally, and those that seem bolted shut. And sometimes God was on both sides of those doors. It is only through discernment and persistence that you know which door to choose.

I had the pleasure of sitting next to Tom Coughlin, president of Wal-Mart. As we were discussing our mutual interest in a Path for Teens project that we were launching in El Paso, Texas, I couldn't help noticing hung on the conference-room wall a number of framed sayings from the founder of Wal-Mart, Sam Walton. Sam believed that there were ten things you needed to do to build a successful business. I had time to jot down the key words from each principle. Here they are, to the best of my memory:

1. Commit to your business.

2. Share your profits with your people.

3. Motivate people to do their best.

4. Communicate what is going on.

5. Appreciate the people who are helping you.

6. Celebrate successes.

7. Listen to people when they speak, especially customers.

8. Exceed expectations.

9. Control expenses better than your competition.

10. Swim upstream.

Item number ten caught my eye: swim upstream.

The wisdom of Sam Walton's philosophies has been proven over time. Wal-Mart is now the largest and most profitable company in the world—employing more than one million people around the globe.

Sam decided that people in middle America had as much right to fine merchandise at reasonable prices as people anywhere else in the world. He decided to serve people in rural America rather than in the metropolises where millions of consumers were located. He felt that farmers and their wives deserved to save a buck and not have to drive all the way into big towns to get their needs met. People at the time scoffed at his concept.

Retail centers were always located around big cities, not in the middle of farm fields. Sam quietly began swimming upstream, starting with a local five-and-dime store that he acquired, turning that into 13 stores, then expanding to 100 stores—always employing his ten principles of success along the way. Today there are 3,400 Wal-Marts across the globe, and the little farm town of Bentonville, Arkansas, houses the largest corporation in America. Sam Walton swam upstream and was a success.

When the Great Depression hit, IBM was only one of many corporations that saw stock prices plummet. Thomas Watson Sr., the CEO of IBM, took the risk of keeping IBM's factories open. He refused to lay off workers and even went so far as to invest millions of dollars in a research and development arm. Author Kevin Maney summed up the story in his book *The Maverick and His Machine: Thomas Watson Sr. and the Making of IBM.*

Maney writes, "Watson borrowed a common recipe for stunning success: one part madness; one part luck; and one part hard work to be ready when luck kicked in." Watson, ever the optimist, took every opportunity to predict the end of the Depression and express his belief that "industrial progress has never stopped." He said that the troubles of America were due not to overproduction but to underproduction, and he positioned IBM to begin manufacturing machines in record numbers at a time when nobody was really ordering any.

Yet then a "miracle" occurred. President Franklin D. Roosevelt signed the Social Security Act into law on August 14, 1935. Suddenly every business in America had to track every employee's hours and wages, and determine what amount needed to be paid into Social Security. The demand was overwhelming—for machines, for accounting systems, for expertise in how to track the details of business. IBM won the contract to do all of FDR's New Deal accounting, and revenues jumped from $19 million in 1934 to $31 million in three years. Tom Watson swam upstream and was rewarded for it.

When you consider the words of Jesus, you will be amazed at how often he asked people to swim upstream. Jesus told the fishermen to undo tradition and throw the net on the other side of the boat. Jesus told Peter later in a dream to take the message of good news to the Gentiles, a message that was changing a tradition of "exclusivity" of nearly three thousand years. Jesus told his disciples to swim upstream, be kind to their enemies, and pray for them. He told his disciples to swim upstream when he declared that they were to seek not the things of the world, which rust and can be stolen, but to seek first the kingdom of God, an invisible state of being, and store up treasures in heaven. Jesus' every message was "swim upstream."

Jesus swam upstream.

QUESTIONS

1. Where is your Coach asking you to swim upstream?

2. What seems so difficult about it?

3. What might be the reward if indeed that is where the treasure lies?

Dear Lord,
Thank you for teaching me that your ways are higher than my ways. Thank you for challenging me not to take the easy way out . . . not to just walk through any door that swings open, but to seek your will and guidance in all things. Amen.

SHOW YOURSELF
FRIENDLY

A MAN WHO HAS FRIENDS MUST
HIMSELF BE FRIENDLY,
BUT THERE IS A FRIEND WHO
STICKS CLOSER THAN A BROTHER.
—PROVERBS 18:24 (NKJV)

Recently a dear friend shared his experience of attending the funeral of a teenage boy who had been tragically killed in an accidental shooting. This boy, who had only lived to be sixteen years old, had no real "accomplishments" to speak of at his funeral. He had not won any awards or honors, or set any records at school. His grades were not particularly outstanding.

Yet his funeral was filled to overflowing. People who came to say good-bye to him were so many in number that they had to stand outside and wait in line to show their respects.

His grief-stricken mother was overwhelmed by the outpouring of love and condolences by the community. Sniffling through her tears, she turned to my friend and said, "A student came up to me and said, 'Billy showed himself friendly to everyone, and that is what we loved about him.'" His gifts were not honors or awards, but a spirit that was open and friendly to others—seeing only good in others, and going beyond himself to acknowledge that.

So many people grew up with an image of an angry, thundering, lightning-scattering God that it is hard for them to imagine God as being friendly. Yet one only has to glance through the Gospels to realize how friendly Jesus really was. He was always reaching out to others and expecting the best from and for them.

"Hi, Zacchacus! Why don't you come down out of that tree and let's have supper together?" he called out good-naturedly to a man that others mocked and scorned. Jesus showed himself friendly.

"Hi, there," he said to the woman at the well. "What are you really looking for here? " He spoke first and in a friendly manner to a perfect stranger. He reached out to her.

Consider his recruiting methods. "Hi, there! Want to follow me?" And they did!

Six days ago I was walking on the Rio Grande riverbank with some friends. We had just returned from church and were enjoying the loveliness of the day. We had gone about a mile when I noticed a dog lying in the bushes. At first I thought it was hurt. One friend with me jumped back in fear because the dog was hidden in the shadows and could easily have reached out and bitten us.

Yet I spoke a kind word to it, and the dog immediately leaped to its feet and came over to me, head down, yet still wagging its tail.

I could see all too clearly the look of abandonment in its eyes. Having worked as a volunteer with Animal Rescue, I realized instantly that this dog had been left out on the river and had been running for days, trying to find its way home. We cupped our hands and poured our water into them, and the shepherd-chow mix gratefully lapped it all up. I took off my red bandanna from around my neck and made a little collar for it, and my friends promptly named him Scooby Doo.

What amazed me about this abandoned dog is that as we continued walking down the ditch, every time he would see a person come around the corner, he would begin to wag his tail. It wasn't as if he recognized the person *per se*. It was that he expected everyone to be worth loving and greeting, even though he had been abandoned. Interestingly enough, this pup's friendliness proved to be his salvation. I was leaving on a plane in exactly one hour and was praying about what to do with this sweet dog. My friends already had two dogs each, and by the arch of their eyebrows, I knew that there wasn't going to be a home for Scooby Doo with them. So, when all else fails, keep walking. We just kept walking while I prayed for an answer.

Suddenly a woman came running alongside us, stopped, and said, "What a beautiful dog!"

I said, "We just found him I think he's been abandoned. Would you like to take him home?" (One can always hope.)

She dropped to her knees, took him in her arms, and said, "Sure."

I was awestruck. "You mean you'll really take him home?"

She said, "Yes! My roommates and I had just decided last night that it was time for us to get a dog. We were going to go to the pound tomorrow and pick one out."

I did a little further interviewing and learned that she was in nursing school. *Perfect— he'll be in good hands*, I thought. So, Scooby Doo licked her face, she took him in her arms, and off the two of them went, walking down the same river-bank that could have been where he died.

There is a spirit of friendliness in the world that is abundant in puppies and lacking in humans. Friendliness isn't just an act; it is an attitude.

I was playing school with Dominique, a five-year-old nephew of a friend of mine. I was the student and he was the teacher, showing me the difference between dimes, nickels, and pennies. I raised my hand and asked, "Teacher, why did they make quarters and dimes silver, while pennies are copper colored?"

Little Dominique put his hands on his hips for a moment while his brow furrowed to consider the answer to the question. A few seconds went by, and then he looked at me and said, "Well, I don't really know why they did that, but I'm sure they meant well by it."

I just hugged him and howled. What a spirit of innocence and friendliness he conveyed.

The very first psalm states, "Blessed are those who do not sit in the seat of scoffers or cynics." Yet haven't we as a society been in danger of that? Friendliness and optimism were hallmarks of Jesus' personality. He was very much willing and able to speak the truth. Yet his resilience and popularity with the crowds showed him to be a friendly man, one who loved to party and celebrate, and bring life wherever he went.

Jesus showed himself friendly.

QUESTIONS

1. When you see a stranger coming around the corner, are you wagging your tail in anticipated friendship, or hunkered down, expecting mistreatment?

2. Where in your life could you be more friendly and reach out to others more than you have been, even in little ways?

3. What might be the benefits of doing that?

Dear Lord,
The fact that the sun rises on the evil as well as the good shows that you are in spirit friendly to all. Help me be the same. Amen.

LEARN TO

LISTEN

BLESSED ARE . . . YOUR EARS
BECAUSE THEY HEAR!
—MATTHEW 13:16 (NJB)

My friend Jane Creswell says that one of the hallmarks of good coaches is that they listen more than they speak. In fact, the ideal ratio of listening to speaking when being a coach is ten to one. In other words, 90 percent of a coach's main activity is listening rather than speaking.

Yes, listening is in such short supply in our society that my mind is racing to retell a story that happened to me just yesterday.

I was in the process of preparing a major presentation to give to a very large company, and I called one of my suppliers to see if they could rush me a sample of something I needed. I was switched to the sales department.

This particular salesman got on the line, heard the first two words out of my mouth, and began to talk . . . and talk . . . and talk. He was one of those people who has perfected the art of never taking a breath while speaking *because taking a breath might mean that there would be a pause in the conversation and a pause in the conversation means that someone else might have a chance to talk and then that really would be a conversation, wouldn't it, rather than a monologue, which is what most people engage in.* (Whew, even there I had to pause and take a breath.)

While he was talking nonstop my cell phone's battery died. I had to get up from my desk in the hotel, run downstairs, and ask the valet to pull up my car, which had the battery recharger in it. When the valet pulled my car up, I hurriedly unlocked the door, opened the suitcase that had the extra cord connector in it, plugged it into the cigarette lighter on my dashboard, hooked up my cell phone to it, looked up the salesman's number in my address book, and called him back. This ordeal took about twelve minutes. When I called him back and he answered the phone, on his second line, he admitted—with surprise—that during that entire time he hadn't even noticed I was gone. "I know," I said quietly, and then he just picked up talking where he'd left off! He didn't even ask what had happened to disconnect us.

I finally told him, "Look, Bill, I've got to go. I'll just e-mail you the information that I need." And that was that.

That man no more realized what I needed than a man in the moon. He just started "selling." When I received the product samples I had ordered, the logo, name, and color were incorrect. As a result, he lost a substantial order, all because he talked instead of listened.

If I were to start a school and design a course on spirituality, the first lessons I would put in Spirituality 101 would be about surrender and listening. In truth, they are one and the same.

You cannot listen when you have an agenda. You cannot listen when you are just waiting for a pause in the conversation so you can insert your opinion. You cannot listen when you presume to know what the problem is before it has even been explored.

I used to do a lot of medical consulting with my advertising agency. I consulted doctors on how to build their medical practices. Research showed that a doctor begins to diagnose a patient within three minutes of walking into the room. Nine out of ten times the doctor interrupts the patient and doesn't even let him complete his sentences! No wonder we have hundreds of thousands of patients dying every year from *iatrogenic* illnesses, which is a very fancy word for "the doctor made a mistake."

My mother is not alone in being disturbed by the level of "dialogue" that is being modeled on talk shows such as

Point and Counterpoint. Nobody gets to finish a sentence. The other person interrupts and keeps escalating the volume until what you have is a shouting match, with nobody being heard or hearing the other party. When you take a position rather than seek the truth, you are in danger of missing the point, counter or otherwise.

Reflective listening takes place when you not only pause and consider what has been said, but are able to repeat it back accurately to the speaker. Reflexive listening is waiting simply for your chance to insert something into the conversation.

The book of Proverbs is full of sayings about the value of silence. One of my favorites is, "Answer not a fool according to his folly" (26:4). In other words, you don't have to express an ignorant opinion just because someone else has.

Jesus was a man of few words. When he walked up to a person on the street, he asked, "What would you like me to do for you?" And then he listened for the answer.

Jesus knew how to listen.

QUESTIONS

1. How much do you really listen to other people?

2. Define *reflective* listening.

3. Define *reflexive* listening.

4. Why is listening a form of surrender?

5. Why is surrender a form of listening?

6. What would the world be like if more people listened rather than shouted at each other?

Dear God,
Jesus said, "Thank you, Father, for listening to me." I want to say the same. Amen.

GET WET

IT WAS AT THIS TIME THAT JESUS CAME
FROM NAZARETH IN GALILEE AND WAS
BAPTISED IN THE JORDAN BY JOHN. AND
AT ONCE, AS HE WAS COMING UP OUT OF THE
WATER, HE SAW THE HEAVENS TORN APART
AND THE SPIRIT, LIKE A DOVE, DESCENDING
ON HIM. AND A VOICE CAME FROM HEAVEN,
"YOU ARE MY SON, THE BELOVED;
MY FAVOUR RESTS ON YOU."
—MARK 1:9–11 (NJB)

Jesus was a man of the desert. He knew that few things in
that arid climate and topography were more valued and

vital than water. Indeed, he described himself as Living Water to the woman at the well.

Water is one of the most mysterious and fascinating elements because it can be reflective and healing, or dangerous and flooding. Some scientists say that water has magnetic properties. Tides follow the pull of the moon, and in one verse we are told that "even the winds and the sea obey him" (Matt. 8:27). Some of Jesus' favorite times were on or around the Sea of Galilee.

Jesus' first miracle was turning water into wine. Yet what amazes me about him was that he was willing to get wet so that we could be lifted high and dry.

When he put his foot into the Jordan River and bowed to be baptized by John, his cousin, he was saying that he was willing to step into a new way of life as well. No more would he be Joseph the carpenter's son. He was about to enter into a new state of being, and of being perceived, and he knew it. He looked at the water and stepped into it, and we were never the same.

One of my favorite passages in scripture is Ezekiel 47. For the purposes of discussion, let's review it here:

> He brought me back to the entrance of the Temple, where a stream flowed eastwards . . . The man went off to the east holding his measuring line and measured off a thousand cubits; he then made me wade across the stream; the water reached my ankles. He measured off another

thousand and made me wade across the stream again; the water reached my knees. He measured off another thousand and made me wade across the stream again; the water reached my waist. He measured off another thousand; it was now a river which I could not cross. (vv. 1–5 NJB)

A precious part of that vision for me is that when Ezekiel steps into the water, at first it is only ankle deep. He is still in control. He can still back out. It is just tickling his ankles. No big deal. But notice how the farther downstream he goes, the deeper the water gets. It goes from being ankle deep to knee deep. And soon it is a river so deep that Ezekiel cannot pass through it.

When you step into God's will, there can be a feeling or perception that you are in control . . . on top of things. God's words and ways are just sort of nibbling at your ankles. You can choose to get out of the stream at this point if you are afraid or the water is too cold or you become uncomfortable.

Yet the deeper you go into God, the deeper the water gets. Pretty soon the water that was a mere stream is carrying you on a journey that you could never have imagined.

I love the story about the Jordan River where the priests are instructed to step into the water.

Yahweh said to Joshua, "This very day, I shall begin to make you great in the eyes of all Israel so that they will know that, as I was with Moses, so I shall be with you. Now, give this order to the priests carrying the ark of the covenant, 'When you have reached the brink of the waters of the Jordan, you must halt in the Jordan itself'" . . . Accordingly, when the people left their tents to cross the Jordan, the priests carried the ark of the covenant ahead of the people. As soon as the bearers of the ark reached the Jordan and the feet of the priests carrying the ark touched the waters . . . the upper waters stood still and formed a single mass over a great distance . . . The priests carrying the ark of the covenant of Yahweh stood firm on dry ground in mid-Jordan, while all Israel crossed on dry ground, until the whole nation had completed its crossing of the Jordan. (Josh. 3:7–8, 14–17 NJB)

Notice that the victorious crossing did not appear until they had gotten their feet wet.

Maybe you remember going out on the high dive, determined to jump into the swimming pool below. Everything looks great at first. It seems that the big kids are having fun doing it. No ambulances have appeared. Your time has come. You walk out onto the diving board, ready to make your Olympic dive, yet suddenly you see the water dripping from your shivering body down, down, down onto the pool below. You freeze. This board is much higher than you thought. You sense pain is your destiny rather than glory. You begin to back up, step by step. But now people are behind you—pounding on the board, calling you names.

You can't turn back now. So, you close your eyes, say a prayer, and then jump. You hit the water with a splash, come up for air with joy and exhilaration, and can't swim to the side fast enough to get back on that board again.

Every new endeavor is like that. There is the kind of courage it takes to get up on the board, and then there is another kind of courage required to jump off it. Yet until you are willing to stretch a little bit and get your feet wet in deeper water, you will not mature.

We are capable of so much more than we think we are. Too often someone sets limits on himself based on what he knows or has known. He decides that this is enough, right here, and he says in essence, "Don't take me any further. Don't show me anything else that is new. Let me stay in my comfort zone." And then he settles in and settles down and never lives to the high glory that was his divine destiny.

Do you know people who don't want their worlds disturbed? Who need to look good and be sure, far more than they need to grow? I know people like that, too, but I tend not to stay around them. In one of my books I refer to them as "stiff necked" people. They can't turn their heads to the left or the right, up or down, to explore new horizons. They stay high and dry, and sort of flake off into the sunset— never having made a difference, never having tasted all of their sorrows or all of their joy.

Jesus was willing to change from one state to another . . . from being a carpenter to a preacher and healer . . . to enter into lands that were not friendly to him, familiar to him, or easy on him. Yet he took that step. He was willing to get wet, and that is when his "reign" began.

QUESTIONS

1. Where are you maneuvering to stay in your comfort zone?

2. What water is swirling around in front of you, stirring up unnamed fears?

3. Who is pounding on the diving board behind you right now wanting a turn on the board?

Dear Lord,
Help me *get wet!* Amen.

RECEIVE CONTINUAL FEEDBACK

ANYONE WHO HAS EARS SHOULD LISTEN!
—MATTHEW 11:15 (NJB)

Recently Keilty, Goldsmith and Company conducted a survey of more than 8,000 employees. The study, led by Marshall Goldsmith, was designed to detect the effectiveness of managers who had attended a leadership develop ment program, as perceived by those who reported directly to them (direct reports). The study was to measure the impact of a learning experience, based on those who should benefit most directly from it. Reported in *The Heart of*

Coaching by Thomas Crane, the study revealed a number of amazing things.

Managers were asked to respond to direct reports and their feedback, implement an improvement plan based on the feedback, and then follow up with the direct reports as to progress that was made. Essentially the more the managers responded to feedback, the more highly they were rated as being successful. Where leaders were asked to respond, but did not follow up, they were seen as actually getting worse in their effectiveness. Leaders who responded and then consistently followed up with their direct reports were perceived as having improved by 95 percent. In other words, the consistent follow-up led to the highest rating of effectiveness.

People need feedback. People crave feedback. Yet all too often business leaders believe that feedback is either

(*a*) negative only—to catch people doing something wrong.

(*b*) given once a year in the form of a performance review.

This thinking totally misses the boat. Once a client or employee or person agrees to the coaching process, then follow-up and feedback need to be given consistently, in the moment.

Just last week I went through a security detector at the airport. I dutifully put my shoes in the gray basket, whipped out my laptop and put it in the gray basket, took off my belt and earrings and put them in the gray basket, and walked through the detector with my arms held exactly two inches from my sides. The woman who was watching the detector screen over my head looked at me, smiled, and said, "Good job." I perked up immediately, responding to the praise of a security guard who somehow had learned that people need feedback, even when going through monotonous and undesired activities.

My friend Shelly Buckner is a master at designing incentive programs for children. When one parent complained that her child was not performing well in kindergarten, Shelly sat down and asked her about the boy's behaviors. The parent said, "He is not standing in line properly, he is not raising his hand at the right time, he is not doing his homework, and he is not picking up his toys." Shelly suggested that the parent buy a small bucket, a deck of Yu-Gi-Oh cards, and ten rubber frogs. She gave these instructions: "Every time Billy does something right, give him a frog to put in the bucket. When he gets all the frogs in the bucket, give him a Yu-Gi-Oh card. Make sure the frogs are awarded according to the task the teacher is asking him to do."

A week later the parent called back. "Billy is behaving wonderfully now. All it seemed to take was the frogs in the bucket. I don't have to yell or nag, and neither does the teacher!"

Shelly told me that kids are usually eager to please—

they just need feedback and incentives that are highly tangible, short term, positive, and immediate.

Feedback can sometimes be self-given. A friend of mine is a top salesperson at a large financial firm. She makes her living by cold calling clients from a list of leads she receives. She consistently earns in the high six figures, even though most of the people on the list hang up on her. When I asked her how she stayed motivated, she told me her secret. She said, "I know that I need to make one hundred calls a day in order to turn up three sales. So, each morning I take out one hundred paper clips and pour them out in a pile on the left side of my phone. Every time I make a call, regardless of the outcome, I get to move one paper clip from the left side of my phone to the right side. My goal each day is to move those paper clips from the left to the right side of the phone. Doing this guarantees that I will make those one hundred calls, no matter what." Sally tapped into her own need for visible and tangible feedback. A pile of paper clips on the right side of her phone told her she had done a good job.

Coaching is the fine art of meeting the need for consistent feedback that is wired into the human brain. Even God gave feedback to Jesus, saying, "This is my beloved Son, in whom I am well pleased." Jesus told of the wealthy man who said to his faithful stewards, "Well done." When his disciples came back to him with their wins and losses, Jesus gave them feedback about how they needed to improve: "This kind only comes out through prayer and fasting." They told him their failures. He gave them feedback.

Jesus, your Coach, will give you feedback.

QUESTIONS

1. Who gives you feedback now regarding your performance?

2. What kind of feedback is it?

3. How could Jesus give you specific feedback?

Dear Lord,

You give me feedback in many ways—through scripture, through friends and family, through pastors and associates, through bosses and coworkers. Help me listen to the ultimate form of feedback that you promised, which is the peace that passes all understanding. I seek to do your will. Amen.

TAKE

ACTION

IT IS NOT ANYONE WHO SAYS TO ME,
"LORD, LORD," WHO WILL ENTER THE KINGDOM
OF HEAVEN, BUT THE PERSON WHO DOES THE
WILL OF MY FATHER IN HEAVEN.
—MATTHEW 7:21 (NJB)

As a person who loves to dream just about more than anything, I have to continually remind myself to take action. I
was blessed early in my life to have a personal coach in the
form of my boss at the YWCA, Catherine Calhoun. When
we met, I was a twenty-eight-year-old dreamer—dreaming

about writing, dreaming about the incredible things God was going to do, dreaming about how someday I would do something amazing, dreaming about how that might look *someday*.

Catherine, who at one time considered becoming a Methodist preacher, took me aside after observing me on the job for some time. She said, "Laurie Beth, I believe that faith is about taking action in the moment, trusting God to guide you—not waiting for miracles to arrive fully formed." She said lovingly, "I'm tired of hearing you talk . . . get out there and start rowing."

Another day she told me, "Writers write."

I said, "What do you mean by that?"

She repeated, "Writers write. They don't talk about writing—they write."

So, I started writing . . . just in my journal, but more diligently than before.

She brooked no excuses when it came to calling procrastination "faith." In fact, like Jesus, she is fairly intolerant of mealymouthed, wishy-washy behavior. Remember that Jesus said, "I know your deeds, that you are neither cold nor hot. I wish you were either one or the other! So, because you are lukewarm . . . I am about to spit you out of my mouth" (Rev. 3:15–16 NIV).

Jesus also said this: "No man, having put his hand to the plough, and looking back, is fit for the kingdom of God" (Luke 9:62). In other words, he was saying, "Get on with it."

Pastor and author Erwin Raphael McManus states much the same thing in his book *Seizing Your Divine Moment*. In it he recounts a story of Jonathan, son of Saul. Saul and his army of six hundred men are engaged in a battle with those pesky Philistines. While both sides are resting, Jonathan and his armor bearer sneak away. Jonathan decides to seize the moment rather than camp under a tree, and he says, "Let's go up there anyway and see what is going on."

The two of them do. They scare up a few of the Philistines and are able to slay them and instill such a panic that the entire army is routed as soon as Saul's army are alerted to it. The point of the story, recounted in 1 Samuel 14:1–23, is that Jonathan decides to seize the moment and take action rather than wait for something to happen.

I have to watch myself or I'll fall into the trap of watching the news all the time. I am reminded of Harvey MacKay, who said, "There are two kinds of people in the world. Those who watch the news, and those who make the news." Those who make the news are people who are seizing the moment in front of them and taking action.

I am continually amazed and dismayed at the number of Christians I meet who say they are "waiting for the Lord to show them his will." I believe that *we* are responsible for discerning the Lord's will, based on our natural gifts and talents, and then taking action toward noble causes. God's will for our lives is often revealed only in retrospect. We take action and then look back and see how everything came together . . . how this person crossing our paths led to this happening, and so forth. God's will for us is so immense, and so complex, that it could never be revealed to us in a FedEx package or an e-mail. We must go out and meet it!

Jesus seized the moment.

QUESTIONS

1. Where are you just waiting for God to act?

2. What if your actions are the paths that miracles need to take in order to come true?

3. How can you know you are doing God's will?

Dear Lord,
Teach me to seize the moment, as Jesus did, and always do good, wherever I find it. Amen.

BE WILLING
TO ASK FOR
HELP

"I AM SO SAD THAT I FEEL AS IF I AM DYING.
STAY HERE AND KEEP AWAKE WITH ME."
—MATTHEW 26:38 (CEV)

Jesus was willing to ask for help. For example, we are all familiar with the times he asked for help from up above: "Dear Lord, hear my prayer. Heal this child," or "Raise Lazarus." He always acknowledged that he needed help from his Father to do anything. Yet he was equally comfortable asking for help from down below, that is, from his earthly peers: "Will you follow me?" or "Will you wait with me?" In both instances he was asking his companions to help him with his emotional struggles—something that most men or leaders would not be comfortable doing. One of the most amazing qualities about Jesus, in fact, was his willingness to show vulnerability.

My friend Linda Miller is in a business partnership with Jane Creswell and Suzanne Goebels. All three of them have expertise in coaching with corporations at the highest level as well as working behind the scenes with congregations and denominations. Linda and I sat down recently to discuss the topic of coaching, not only from a Christian perspective, but also from a corporate perspective.

Linda shared that one of the biggest misconceptions about coaching is that people feel they have to know all the answers. "The last thing you want to see from a coaching perspective are people who think they have all the answers. When people go into coaching because they really have a desire to teach, they don't make good coaches at all. Coaches don't teach; they facilitate. Coaches don't tell; they draw forth. And coaches are willing to admit when they don't know the answers." In fact, in a difficult conversation that she and I had regarding a mutual consulting arrangement, Linda said, "I will be the first to tell you when my expertise has run out, and we need to draw in some new wisdom." Her willingness to be vulnerable made me trust her all the more.

In contrast, I worked with a man who claimed to be the guru in his particular endeavor. When I asked some probing questions, it didn't take long to discover that he was not well versed in the areas where I truly needed help. However, he didn't tell me that. My gut did.

Jesus spoke the truth at all times so that people could trust him. His willingness to ask for help . . . to show vulnerability . . . is yet another reason people were so willing to follow him. He indicated that he had a need for them in his life, and that allowed them the terrific feeling of being needed.

I remember standing in a tour in the famous Louvre art museum in France. Feeling thrilled to be there, I took notes on what was being said. The docent told us that the Impressionist masters made their living not from painting "masterpieces" so much as doing commissions—that is, painting what their patrons wanted, which were usually portraits.

One of the most influential artists was Jan van der Meer from Holland. While other artists from the same period might have become famous for this or that particular painting, his was called the age of Van der Meer. He ushered in an entrepreneurial spirit that excited all of Europe.

He always left a little bit of a commissioned piece unfinished. When the patron came to review the final work, he or she would say, "Oh, my, you forgot to put the button on that collar." Van der Meer would then make a flurry and say,

"Oh, my, I can't believe I missed that. What a great eye you have." He then would paint in the button while the patron stood there. The effect was that the patrons felt that they had made a significant contribution to the piece. They then took ownership and bought the painting without making other major adjustments.

Although you might feel that doing this was manipulative on Van der Meer's part, I see it as a stroke of genius. He was, in effect, asking for help. People were so glad to give it that they left feeling wonderful, while he left feeling richer in every way.

Not too long ago there was an extraordinary story of the woman physician who had taken up residence in the Antarctic on a small exploratory station there. No one was able to get in or out of the station for months during that time of the year because of the weather. She was doctor to two hundred people and prided herself on always being in charge and in command of her field of expertise. One day while showering she noticed a lump in her breast. Unwilling at first to admit to her coworkers that she might have cancer, she kept measuring the lump quietly on her own until it was clear that it was growing—and fast. She confided finally in one of the more gruff people on the team, who told her that she must share with the others her predicament. When she did, it was both exciting and poignant to see the team's creativity in wanting to help her.

Offers for help ranged from giving her shots to trying

to catapult her to a hovering helicopter. Ultimately she and her team did a biopsy, which determined that the cells were indeed malignant. The team was able to use a satellite connection and patch in advice from other physicians about how to treat the disease until the next flight could get in to airlift her to the United States for medical treatment.

The biggest lesson that this independent doctor learned was how helpful people can be when they are asked and given the opportunity. The love from the team truly "airlifted her" to safety.

A pastor I know wanted a mural painted on the side of a relatively ugly wall on the church grounds. He hired a local muralist to sketch in the overall painting, and then he requested that the congregants and their children fill in the "paint by numbers" sketch.

I will never forget a six-year-old coming up to me and saying, "Laurie Beth, come over here and see my painting." I went with him as he proudly pointed to the little green frog sitting at the edge of the painted-on pond. "I painted that frog," the child crowed. His eyes were bright with excitement as he took ownership for his three-inch green-bellied portion of the pond. Because the pastor had been wise enough to ask for help, and give credit where it was due, he got a mural in which the entire congregation took pride and felt ownership.

God was open enough and vulnerable enough to ask Adam to help him name the animals in the Garden. Perhaps he hoped that if humans felt some ownership of the creation, we might feel more involved and responsible for it. (The end of that "dominion" relationship remains to be seen.)

Yet even God was there displaying a need and desire for teamwork—for a combined effort and contribution to a larger whole.

Know-it-alls are annoying to everyone, even and especially to God.

Jesus asked for help.

QUESTIONS

1. When and where have you recently asked for help?

2. Was it a large or a small project?

3. What might be five benefits of being willing to ask for help with the challenge facing you now?

Dear Lord,
Help me get over my pride enough to realize that some portion of my painting is missing. Help me ask for help from others to see what it is, that we all may feel the richer for it. Amen.

THINK

INSIDE

THE SOLUTION

GOD SAID, LET THERE BE LIGHT:
AND THERE WAS LIGHT.
—GENESIS 1:3

Not too long ago a friend of mine bravely stepped up to volunteer for his company's blood drive. He warned the woman putting the needle in that he had a tendency to get woozy. Apparently she didn't hear him or didn't believe him because she just jabbed away as if he was a normal person.

Everything went fine until it was time for him to stand up. When he tried to stand, his knees buckled and he went down, hitting his head on the edge of the desk. That caused even more blood to spurt, requiring an emergency call to 911 and an ambulance ride to the hospital. When all was said and done, my friend's good deed of giving blood cost him about $1,500 in emergency care.

Knowing that my family, too, has a history of similar experiences, I went reluctantly to have my blood drawn. For some reason, they only had student nurses on duty. I took one look at Monica's braces, freckles, and lunch box, and politely requested to have an experienced nurse draw my blood. "No offense," I said to the apparent teenager, "I just want someone to get it right the first time."

So, over came Connie, an obviously more experienced nurse, who sat down and said, "Clench your fist for me."

I did so, closing my eyes, trying to imagine myself somewhere on a beach far away. But unfortunately all I kept feeling was jab, jab, jab! For some reason Connie could not find a "portal." My arm was becoming a pincushion.

Finally I heard Monica say, "My professor said we were to think inside the vein." Monica sat down, studied my arm for a moment, closed her eyes, and the needle slipped in.

It was a painful but memorable lesson. Connie was jabbing *at* the vein. Only when Monica thought *inside* the vein, could she find the solution to the problem.

When Jesus looked at the man with the withered hand,

did he see the withered hand? I often ask this question in seminars, and people hesitate to answer, thinking it is a trick question.

The answer is obvious. Of course Jesus saw the withered hand, or he wouldn't have known that healing needed to take place. But he thought inside the whole hand, and that led to its transformation.

I'm trying this piece of advice with some challenges I am facing. Frankly I am looking at my own inadequacies regarding something I am feeling called to do. I'm wondering now if instead of looking at my weaknesses, I should "think inside the Vine" and realize how naturally the solutions will flow as I stay connected to my Source.

They say an acorn has to move the equivalent of ten tons of earth in order to see its first daylight sprout above ground. Would it have made it if it looked at the problem?

Jesus said, "The kingdom of God is within you" (Luke 17:21). He also said, "I am the vine, you are the branches" (John 15:5 NJB). Natural connection. Easy flow. Why do we make things so hard?

Jesus thought inside the solution, which is where we always are.

QUESTIONS

1. Where in your life are you looking at the problem rather than thinking from inside the solution?

2. How often do you see yourself as being separate from God?

3. Where is your ego in terms of the "problem"?

4. If you didn't have an ego, would there really be a "problem"?

Dear Lord,
Help me understand how natural solutions flow as long as I remind myself where I am and where I am meant to be. Amen.

MAINTAIN A SENSE OF WONDER

SING TO HIM, MAKE MUSIC FOR HIM,
RECOUNT ALL HIS WONDERS!
—PSALM 105:2 (NJB)

As I prepare for my day, I often listen to Christian television shows. I like the music programs the most, being fully
convinced that if we all sang more and talked less, the world
would be more heavenly. Yesterday I overheard a man
singing a Christmas song with the words "my heart is lost in

the ten tiny fingers of this baby's hands." What a simple and poetic way to describe the vulnerability, the vastness, the wonder of a personal relationship with Jesus! We who think we know and see so much give our lives to Someone who saw the world through a baby's eyes and leads us like a child.

Yesterday while shopping I saw a holiday gag gift: a set of shot glasses with eye charts on them. I laughed at the notion, as obviously have others, that people could drink straight shots of alcohol and then evaluate how clearly they were seeing things. In our society today we are constantly being overdosed with medications, media, negative news, and regular doses of threats and fears of terrorism. How clearly are we really seeing our world? When we look at our lives, what do we see? What does Jesus see?

Jesus cares because Jesus sees. And he teaches us to see. Not just what is going on around us . . . not just the daily parade of calendar items and to-do list check-off sheets . . . but the wondrousness of creation.

A friend in Dallas named Beau says that he is convinced that his purpose in life is to "simply be amazed." The world is full of so many wondrous things and events, but if we fail to stop and notice them, our lives are deadened indeed.

I remember being with my godson Jacob the first time he heard thunder. We were all seated around the dinner table, chatting away, when suddenly there was this huge, slow-moving, thunderous boom that literally shook the house as it moved over us. Jacob, who was about two years old at the time, looked at me with the widest eyes. His mouth formed an almost cartoonlike "O" as his child's mind struggled to assimilate this new phenomenon of sound. His wonder made us all stop and ponder anew how magnificent is our God.

One of my hobbies is landscape photography, and I find many incredible scenes to photograph just outside my door. Outside almost any door, miracles abound. Yet do we stop and recognize them . . . capture them . . . embrace them . . . celebrate them? Or do we just plow through, getting to the next dot on our connect-the-dots calendar?

Therapist and author Gay Hendricks uses the phenomenon of wonder as a therapeutic tool. He asserts that if we approached life more with a sense of "wonder," and less with a sense of "having to know, judge or decide," life would be much easier on us.

Author Thomas More states the same thing in his book *Care of the Soul.* According to More, the human soul is so complex and eternal that its needs are beyond fathoming. Why do we think we can harness, box, snare, bend, control, and package it?

There are two main weaknesses I sense in current Christian theology. One is believing that we can take any situation and put a bow or two of scripture around it and have it "solved." The other is thinking that we can take the vastness of God and put I AM in a building or a box.

A delightfully fun friend of mine named Robin and I attended a Christian motivational seminar. We sat through several speakers, then took a break, agreeing that if we heard one more "three points to a happy ending" take on "Candy Cane Christianity," we were going to gag. We went back to hear a speaker who shared her tale of her tragic life. Her tale was so lacking in happy endings that we walked out of the seminar with our heads down. We looked at each other silently for a few moments, and then both of us said at the same time, "Bummer." At dinner we agreed that the only theology that ultimately makes sense is that of relationship over rules, and vastness over immediacy.

Jesus didn't deny the existence of tears, the pain of death, or the sorrow of loss. He looked at it and through it.

He capped everything with a sense of wonder—of knowing that God's love was in and through it all—the underpainting on the canvas that would ultimately shine through. He taught, with every singing breath, that God's love is the creator and finisher and companion on life's wondrous journey.

So, your heart . . . where is it? Is it all bound up and constricted with the demands of the day? Or are you willing to take it, pumping complex mess that it is, and place it into the fingers of a tiny baby's hands?

Jesus taught us the meaning of wonder.

QUESTIONS

1. Have you forgotten a sense of wonder in your life?

2. What situation that is seeming to paralyze you right now might be seen differently if you looked at it with a sense of wonder rather than fear?

3. What would it mean for you to give your life into the hands of a child—to begin to see your world through a child's eyes?

Dear Lord,
You continually marveled at creation—the lilies of the field, the dew on the grass, the fields ripe for harvest. Help me to see the world through a child's eyes today—with a sense of joy and wondrous participation in, and appreciation of, this incredible world—this incredible life. Amen.

REMOVE THE CHIP FROM YOUR SHOULDER

DON'T WALK AROUND WITH A
CHIP ON YOUR SHOULDER.
—PROVERBS 3:30 (*THE MESSAGE*)

The phenomenon of road rage so prevalent in our culture today probably has less to do with traffic entanglements and more to do with chips on our shoulders. Although I could find no dictionary definition of *chips on shoulders*, I have seen it often and probably so have you. I define it as "irrational pent-up hostility that can manifest unexpectedly at inopportune times." This need we have to feel superior to others and/or separate from them leads to such cultural ills as gangs, wars, sexism, racism, discrimination, and just plain stupidity. (Indeed, some philosophers say that racism is really classism in disguise.)

In order to have an abundant life, one must have clear vision and a full, free range of motion, emotionally, spiritually, physically, and mentally. Jesus was constantly working to remove chips from shoulders among his disciples and those he taught.

"Do you think you are better than the Samaritans? Forget it."

"Do you think that a widow's mite is less than your many dollars? Forget it."

"Do you think that a person who spends money on perfume is less worthy than someone who claims to give it to the poor? Forget it." (This woman knew the difference between *pour* and *poor*.)

"Do you think that you can get to heaven with your heart full of judgment and anger? Forget it. God doesn't even want to see you in the temple until you have dealt with the chip on your shoulder."

Jesus calls for a rigorous "full body scan" in order to set you free. If you haven't experienced the new technology of a full body scan, I recommend it. For my annual checkup last year I bit the bullet and paid the thousand dollars to get a glimpse of my innards—all of them. It was an amazing experience to have a technician sit with me and look at the photographic history of my insides.

"Hmmm," said my technician as she scanned the first slide. "Did you ever have mononucleosis?"

"Yes, I did. How did you know?" I asked.

"There is some scarring on this lymph node here. See it?"

"But that happened when I was in my teens," I exclaimed.

"The body remembers everything," said the tech, as we then proceeded slide by slide down to my coccyx, which happens to be fine, thank you very much.

My mother went to the doctor for treatment of a persistent cough, and tests revealed that she had scarring on her heart from having had a heart attack two or three years prior—one that she didn't even know about! "The heart remembers everything," said her doctor in a clinical, if not philosophical, tone.

If you will permit me to make a leap from the medical to the philosophical, chips on shoulders come from scars—little wounds or hurts that we experience and fail to resolve. The wound becomes hard and can gravitate in many directions. It can move up to our eyes and blind us with rage. It can harden our hearts. It can stiffen our necks. And for the purposes of this particular chapter, it can gravitate to chips on our shoulders . . . little, tiny, invisible attitudes that prevent us from being and seeing whole.

Having been raised in a town that is 87 percent Hispanic, I have been adoringly saturated in the Hispanic culture. One day my mother and I were having a discussion with a friend of ours who happens to have been born in Mexico. There was an item on the news about some Hispanics being offended by the Chihuahua mascot being used to promote a Mexican food chain. Apparently a number of people felt the ad was degrading to their culture. As Mom and I discussed the pros and cons of this viewpoint, we asked this particular Hispanic woman how she felt about it. To our surprise, she made a double entendre joke: "Oh, I think Jesus is the only one of us who should have a 'sheep' on his shoulder." We all burst into laughter at her good-natured observation.

Indeed, Jesus is the only one of us who should have a "sheep" on his shoulder, but all too many of us do.

Jesus will remove the chip from your shoulder.

QUESTIONS

1. Where do you have a chip on your shoulder? As a clue to discovering where it is, what triggers you suddenly into an inappropriate rage?

2. What group or groups of people have hurt you in the past? How might that have caused you not to see clearly others who look like them?

3. Are you willing to submit to a spiritual "full body scan" with Jesus? If so, when?

Dear Lord,
Right now, sit with me and look into my heart. Help me clear out old scars from the past, and give me a new heart and new eyes to view every person, every situation, with a fresh perspective of hope, optimism, and the clarity of your all-encompassing love. Amen.

GIVE NO WEIGHT
TO NEGATIVE THOUGHTS

HOW BLESSED IS ANYONE WHO REJECTS THE
ADVICE OF THE WICKED, AND DOES NOT TAKE
A STAND IN THE PATH THAT SINNERS TREAD,
NOR A SEAT IN COMPANY WITH CYNICS, BUT
WHO DELIGHTS IN THE LAW OF YAHWEH
AND MURMURS HIS LAW DAY AND NIGHT.
—PSALM 1:1–2 (NJB)

Many of us may think that the "positive thinking" trend began with motivators such as Dale Carnegie and Zig Ziglar. Yet one only has to read through the Gospels to realize that Jesus emphasized and lived by the rule of positive thinking. Of all people he knew the importance of disciplining the human mind, and he constantly insisted that people audit, examine, and control their thoughts in order to live abundantly. "As you believe, you shall receive" is a thought he emphasized time and again (Mark 11:24).

It is said that we have about sixty thousand thoughts per day—most of them random, many of them negative, and all too many of them similar to the thoughts we had the day before. Basically our brains carry on repetitive, one-sided conversations.

Scientists are learning that the brain actually has grooves in it that come from repeated thinking. That is why a thought becomes an action, and an action becomes a habit, and a habit becomes a pattern of behavior that is almost automatic. It is somewhat like a drop of water that makes its way down a windowpane until it is joined by another drop of water of similar weight, the two of them join a cluster of water droplets, and then you have a rivulet that becomes a stream. You'll notice (you students of rivulets) that the single drop moves more slowly than the rivulets of water. Thoughts, like drops of water, seek the path of least resistance.

Thoughts do not edit themselves. They "go with the flow," as it were, and are attracted to thoughts that look like them, if you will. Hence, negative thoughts attract other negative thoughts.

This lesson on thought is basic, for only when we

understand the significance of the way the mind works, can we begin to change our behaviors.

Jesus was no stranger to negative thinking. In the gospel accounts of his wilderness experience, we are told that the devil tempted him: "If you are really as powerful as you say you are, why not throw yourself off the temple?"

Given that Jesus was obviously hungry and thirsty and faint from his forty-day fast, it is no wonder that negative thoughts began to rush into his mind. Notice how he immediately rebuked each one, using prememorized positive thoughts of scripture to combat the negativity: "You shall not tempt the Lord your God."

When Peter later suggested to him that he should not go to Jerusalem (and meet his destiny) but take an easier way out, Jesus immediately rebuked the thought, recognizing that the negativity came from only one source, and it wasn't God.

> Then he began to teach them that the Son of man was destined to suffer grievously, and to be rejected by the elders and the chief priests and the scribes, and to be put to death, and after three days to rise again; and he said all this quite openly. Then, taking him aside, Peter tried to rebuke him. But, turning and seeing his disciples, he rebuked Peter and said to him, "Get behind me, Satan! You are thinking not as God thinks, but as human beings do." (Mark 8:31–33 NJB)

They say that meditation is one of the hardest skills for human beings to learn, mostly because we are prone to "monkey mind" chatter. Thoughts seem to bubble up or attack from nowhere. The more one tries to still them, the more they rebel. The verse "Be still, and know that I am God" (Ps. 46:10) contains more power than we can imagine—yet few of us are still.

I am amazed at some of the thoughts that appear in my mind—often when I least expect them or am thinking about something else. When a negative or fear-based thought occurs to me, I have developed the habit of wiping it away with a single word. For me, that word is *Beloved*. It is a replacement or reinsertion of the knowledge that "I am my Beloved's, and he is mine." I repeat the word *Beloved* to myself several times to reconnect with God and reassure myself that even though the thought came up, I don't have to add any weight to it.

Once I had a dream where I was wading in a river full of snakes floating by me. I made it to the other side by not panicking and certainly by not picking up any of the snakes. Negative thoughts are like snakes. If you let them float past you, you'll be okay. But if you grab them and try to wrestle with them, you're in for some long time.

Dealing with negative thinking isn't denial. Some thoughts are reality based, particularly where physical safety or common sense is concerned. Yet much of what we think and process is random distraction that channels into primitive bases of fear that ultimately paralyze us and keep us from becoming all that we can be.

A delightful nun named Sister Mary Margaret Funk, whom I met in Indiana, shared with me that the desert saints grouped "afflicting thoughts" into the following categories:

Thoughts about the body: food, sex, and things.

Thoughts about the mind: anger, dejection, and depression.

Thoughts about the soul: spiritual fatigue, vain glory, and pride.

They believed the three best ways to overcome negative thoughts were through direct combat, replacement thoughts, or mantras such as the rosary.

Jesus dealt with negative thoughts through scripture, prayer, and surrender of himself to God. He also demonstrated the wisdom and benefits of having a fun and interesting support group and community of friends.

If you are besieged by negative thoughts, consider the benefits of all of the above, lest the negative thoughts pull you under.

Jesus gave no weight to negative thoughts.

QUESTIONS

1. How many negative thoughts do you have per day? Per hour?

2. How much do you dwell on them?

3. How might you unburden yourself from these kinds of thoughts?

4. What scriptures or wisdom texts might help combat negative thinking?

Dear Lord,
Help me to be a guardian of my thoughts. Let me not give them weight or substance, lest they become a dark cloud keeping me from the joy and sun of your reality. Amen.

FULFILLMENT

There is a subtle but significant difference between success and fulfillment.

When Jesus called out to the fishermen, "Follow me, and I will make you fishers of men," he was redefining success for them. Life under his tutelage was not going to be about increasing an earthly catch (although they certainly did that, too). Jesus' goal for you is a life fully lived. He will call forth in you more love than you ever thought you could handle—more faith than you ever thought was possible—more excitement than any roller-coaster ride you ever took.

People pay to get frightened at movies or deliberately take stimulants to get their adrenaline going. With Jesus as your Coach you won't need drugs to get high. Nor will you need to go to the movies to get frightened. This loving Coach will bring your greatest fears into the light and help turn them into stepping-stones. He will cause you to face your unfaceable issues so that you can see light as well as *be* light.

No longer will you need to wonder whether your glass is half full or half empty. It will be full to overflowing—with joy and contentment and "the peace that passes understanding."

I remember when I first felt called to go out into the desert to write the book *Jesus, CEO*. It was a book that many were warning me *not* to write, yet it was a book that I couldn't help writing. I spent many days staring out at the ocean from my home in San Diego. I also lay awake many nights, pondering how my comfortable life would change if I took the step that loomed before me. The period of deciding was immensely uncomfortable.

It was not smooth or easy or even very graceful. Yet I will never forget the way I felt when I finally settled into my little trailer in the desert, set up my computer, and began to write. I can only describe it like this. I felt like I was nursing my firstborn child. The contentment and joy . . . the feeling of connection and purpose . . . had never been so rich, so deep, or so real. I finally knew what it felt like to feel fulfilled.

When I released myself into the life to which I had been

called, those moments of fulfillment went from being moments, to days, to weeks, to months, to years. Since I have become clear about my mission, and try to live daily in connection and alignment with it, fulfillment is my constant companion. I can finally relate to what the psalmist David wrote, "Surely goodness and mercy shall follow me all the days of my life: and I will dwell in the house of the LORD for ever" (Ps. 23:6).

Fulfillment has many facets to it. In the following section, we will explore some of them.

HAVE NEW
STORIES

I WILL OPEN MY MOUTH AND TELL STORIES.
—MATTHEW 13:35 (*THE MESSAGE*)

An organization in New York hired me to help it and its employees move forward on a new initiative after having just issued a round of layoffs. Given that the decision makers had the choice of any number of companies to help them, I asked the executive who hired me, "Why me?" He said, "Because you are a storyteller, and we need you to tell us a new story about who we are."

I'd never heard a more eloquent, or profound, appeal.

This leader knew that we live according to our stories, and if the story we're living isn't a great one, we can change it.

Jesus did that with the woman at the well. She came during the heat of the day because she was a social outcast. Her story was that she was a "fallen woman," and she was basically going where she would not be seen or taunted. She had bought into the town's version of who she was. Yet Jesus looked at her and saw her old story hovering around her. When he said, "Where is your husband?" he was letting her know that he was aware that she didn't have one. (Old story.) Then he talked about her thirst, which went beyond any need for a drink or a man, but emanated from her very soul: "If you knew who was talking to you right now, you would ask him for a drink of Living Water and know that you will never be thirsty again." (New story.) She went from believing that she was an outcast to someone who ran back in the middle of the day and recruited the whole town to come and see him.

Perhaps no entity has been as effective at changing lives as Alcoholics Anonymous (AA). People come to AA meetings when they are at their depths of despair. They walk in with their old stories. The very first step involves admitting that they are powerless, and they have come to believe that a Higher Power can help free them from their addictions. They walk in feeling alone (old story) and walk out with a new Higher Power on their side (new story).

Virtually all therapy involves helping clients associate

new meanings with old stories. Whether it is Gestalt or rational emotive or Freudian, many, if not most, types of therapy involve someone listening to an old story and helping the client find new meanings in it. Only when the person has transferred from believing the old story (I am a victim) to believing a new story (this event is only helping me be a much stronger person) does real healing take place.

Our cultures and our families tell us stories about ourselves. A friend of mine shared with me that she had returned to her hometown and was greeted by her young sister whom she had baby-sat when the youngster was only three to five years old. Allison had become the state tennis champion at her high school, set a number of athletic records, then fell into drug use and scuffles with the law before giving her life to Christ. Her young sister took Allison aside and said, "I decided that I was going to become just like you. I, too, became the state tennis champion, and wherever there was an athletic record posted with your name on it, I either matched or beat it. I figured it was in my genes." But Allison was astonished to learn that her sister had also drifted into drugs and trouble with the law, "just like you did," said the young woman. Allison then took her aside and shared with her a new story, about her new life with Christ. Allison sat there in amazement as she shared with me how her sister had literally walked in her footsteps, believing that her story was Allison's story, and vice versa.

This is also an example of a self-obtained and then self-fulfilled prophecy. The girl believed "the story of Allison" and lived it out, believing that she was genetically "born" to do so.

In the book *How Customers Think* by Gerald Zaltman, he writes that the words *store* and *story* are very similar for a reason. The mind remembers what it attaches emotion to, and by incorporating stories around facts or perceptions, the memory improves. In fact, memory gurus teach people to help remember names by telling a story around a person's name. It is a time-honored technique to link stories to memory. Do we understand that the stories we tell ourselves, about ourselves, often tend to come true?

The truth is, you and I are playing out on a daily basis the stories we believe about ourselves. Which story is that?

QUESTIONS

1. Based on your life results right now, which story about yourself have you been living?

2. Do you believe that you could get—and live out—a new story?

Dear Lord,
I think I want to hear a new story at bedtime tonight. Tell me the story about me—why I was created and where you would like to see me go. I can't wait to hear it. Amen.

IMPROVE YOUR

SELF-ESTEEM

I WILL MAKE YOU AN OBJECT OF ETERNAL PRIDE,
A SOURCE OF JOY FROM AGE TO AGE.
—ISAIAH 60:15 (NJB)

One of the joys and challenges of having Jesus as your personal Coach is the work he will do on and with your self-esteem.

There seem to be two schools of thought on the issue of self-esteem for Christians—those who believe that they are worth nothing because they were born in sin, and those who believe that they are worth everything because they were born in blessing. I have been familiar with both styles and approaches, and I lean more toward the latter.

Some people go to extremes when it comes to self-esteem and the lack thereof. I am reminded of the preacher who gave a wonderful sermon on Sunday. As the crowd was leaving, many of them were complimenting him on his words. When a ten-year-old girl came up and said, "I really enjoyed your sermon, Reverend," he leaned down and said, "Oh, it wasn't me, honey, it was *God!*" She stood there for a moment, looked up at him, and said, "It wasn't *that* good!"

Just yesterday I spoke with a man who said the Holy Spirit gave him an idea and told him he was not supposed to take credit for it. Yet four times during the conversation he brought up the "don't take the credit" words from the Holy Spirit, which of course makes me think that this guy was very much—although subtly—trying to take credit for it. And in the words of the little girl, it was good, but it wasn't *that good.*

In my seminars on *Jesus, CEO,* I challenge people to find anything negative that Jesus ever said about himself. No one has yet been able to produce a word. He was able to separate the behavior of the person from the essence of the person, which is why he was able to so freely love "sinners." He told his friends that he called them brothers and sisters, not lesser beings. He told them that they would do greater things than he was doing. He told them that they had the faith within them to accomplish *anything* if they asked it believing.

I also ask people in my seminars to remember and write down a positive prophecy that they have received. Invariably nearly 30 percent of the audience will say that no one has ever given them a positive prophecy. That makes me wonder if they have read the Gospels lately, and if they did read them, did they take any of Jesus' words to heart? He said, "Whoever believes in me will perform the same works as I do myself, and will perform even greater works," and "If you ask me anything in my name, I will do it" (because I love and cherish you that much!) (John 14:12, 14 NJB).

Jesus believes that you and he can do anything together. Your faith, *combined with his power and his faith in you*, can truly move mountains and release wonderful forces of blessing on this earth.

One reason that coaching is showing such phenomenal returns on investment is the simple dynamic of having another person believing in you and moving alongside you with that belief.

◆ Jesus sees you as wholly loved and beautiful.

◆ Jesus wants you to see yourself as he does.

◆ Jesus will believe in you, even when you can't.

QUESTIONS

1. Who do you think you are?

2. Who do you think Jesus thinks you are?

3. What have you attracted into your life through your positive and negative beliefs about yourself?

Dear Lord,
Help me to see myself as you see me. Help me to feel as loved as I truly am. Amen.

BE A VOICE, NOT AN ECHO

LET ME HEAR YOUR VOICE.
—SONG OF SONGS 2:14 (NJB)

As I rounded the curve heading down to the freeway, I noticed a campaign poster stuck in somebody's front yard. It read, "Vote for Susan. She Will Be a Voice, Not an Echo." I love that line.

Jesus was a man whose life changed history not only because he was the Son of God, but also because his was a unique voice, not an echo. He did not just perpetuate the way things were done.

He said, "Do it differently." He did not just remind others what had been said in the past. He said, "Behold, I show you a new way of doing things . . . things that have never been done before."

Many of us have lost our voices. We have surrendered them to television and radio and the endless array of talking heads on boxed-in portions of TV screens that tell us what we should be thinking. Little crawl lines now perpetually feed us information about the perceived state of the world around us. It seems to me that for every one person talking, there are thirty shoving microphones in that person's face and asking, "Tell us something we don't already know."

In a workbook my friend Catherine loaned me about empowering teams, there is a cartoon of a group of people marching down a wide road. Just above their shoulders, in the upper right-hand corner, is a person who is dressed like the others but is pointing a different direction. He is waving and trying to get their attention so that they will see this new road he has found. Yet the masses keep marching down the same old road. The implication is that waving alone won't get the job done—you have to use your voice.

My friend Doug Hawthorne is CEO of Texas Health Resources (THR), a $1 billion health care system that was created through a strategic merger of thirteen faith-based hospitals in the Dallas–Fort Worth metroplex. Doug has been somewhat of a mentor for me, even as I am officially a consultant to him and the organization in matters of spirituality.

When THR was created, the system had a deficit of $20 million. Within two years Doug and his team of 15,000 employees had turned that into a $20 million positive income line. The next year the positive cash flow was $36 million, and last year it was an astounding $93 million—all while delivering indigent care and dealing with the same set of variables other hospitals have to deal with.

Doug believes and teaches that everything is built around mission and relationships. While some nonprofit hospitals say, "No margin, no mission," Doug's mantra is, "No mission, no margin." In other words, if you *are* living your mission, you *will* make a profit. Others say, "If you can't make a profit, you won't have a mission." Doug puts the cart in the right place.

He communicates with his staffers through a variety of ways. One of my favorites is the hot line "Yo Doug," which any employee can call anytime. I asked him if people really use it, and he said, "Yes, they do. But not as often as you might think. Knowing that they have a voice, and that it will be heard, helps them relax and concentrate more on their particular duties. It is wonderful."

I was actually in his office when someone called on the hot line and asked if he could recommend a good podiatrist for the caller's mother. Doug smiled and asked Tina, his assistant, to look up the names of several in the area close to the employee. One might think that a CEO of a $1 billion enterprise has better things to do with his time than answer random phone calls. But Doug has built the success of the enterprise on caring and listening to each person's voice.

He has a drawing in his office that is a commissioned art piece. It shows a group of cars heading down a road between tall mountains. One highway sign marks the road to success. Along the way are road markers such as "Value other people's time" and "Communicate constantly." Another sign points toward the status quo. From the viewer's standpoint it is obvious that up ahead are many hazards—falling rocks and careening trucks. The message of the art piece is clear. By staying on the road to valuing other people's time, and communicating, one can avoid the obstacles. The piece tells me that Doug is a leader who has chosen to be a voice for new ways of doing things rather than an echo of the status quo.

I was thrilled recently when I learned that a woman attending one of our Path Training Seminars was a former press secretary to a governor. She said she realized one day that she was being paid to be someone else's voice to the public. She is now preparing to find her own voice, in hopes of someday running for governor herself.

Finding your voice can take a lifetime or a moment. But once you do, use it.

In one of the most moving passages in Song of Songs, the lover says to the other, "Let me hear your voice" (Song 2:14 NKJV). *Your* voice. He wasn't interested in hearing someone else's. He wants to hear *yours*.

QUESTIONS

1. Where are you an echo?

2. Where are you a voice?

3. What is the danger of merely repeating information that others have fed into you?

4. How did Jesus express a voice unique enough to change the course of history?

5. How will you?

Dear Lord,
Help me find my voice and use it for your glory. Amen.

LEARN OF
YOUR DIVINE
CONNECTION

WHITHER SHALL I FLEE FROM THY PRESENCE?
—PSALM 139:7

My mission is to recognize, promote, and inspire divine connection in myself and others. The more I have contemplated and endeavored to live this mission, the more of an oxymoron it becomes because *connection* implies "separateness."

And the more I grow in God, the less separate I feel. Jesus said, "Apart from me, you can do nothing." He was speaking of the need for, and naturalness of, divine connection.

Listen to King David's take on connection in Psalm 139:

Yahweh, you examine me and know me,
you know when I sit, when I rise,
you understand my thoughts from afar.
You watch when I walk or lie down,
you know every detail of my conduct.
A word is not yet on my tongue
before you, Yahweh, know all about it . . .
Where shall I go to escape your spirit?
Where shall I flee from your presence?
If I scale the heavens you are there,
if I lie flat in Sheol, there you are.
If I speed away on the wings of the dawn,
if I dwell beyond the ocean,
even there your hand will be guiding me,
your right hand holding me fast . . .
You created my inmost self,
knit me together in my mother's womb.
For so many marvels I thank you;
a wonder am I, and all your works are wonders.
You knew me through and through,
my being held no secrets from you,
when I was being formed in secret,
textured in the depths of the earth . . .

In your book all my days were inscribed,
every one that was fixed is there.
How hard for me to grasp your thoughts,
how many, God, there are!
If I count them, they are more than the grains of sand;
if I come to an end, I am still with you . . .
God, examine me and know my heart,
test me and know my concerns.
Make sure that I am not on my way to ruin,
and guide me on the road of eternity. (vv. 1–18, 23–24 NJB)

God is omnipotent and omnipresent. We are the ones whose forms are temporary and changing.

A friend of mine who is a messianic Jew attended a kabala meeting in New York. He said the men in the room were standing and chanting, with arms in the air, "God, give us immortality! God, give us immortality!"

My friend said he just sat there watching with an amused expression. When the chanting finally stopped, several of the men came over to him and demanded to know why he hadn't joined in the chant. He said, "Because we already are immortal. It was Jesus' gift to us, and it still holds true."

What does it mean to be immortal—to live beyond our flesh?

Not too long ago I was approached by a group that is stretching my imagination of what is possible. This group is imagining a children's village, which will contain pavilions of spiritual "edutainment" displays. I have been invited to participate by designing a pavilion specifically around my teachings on Jesus. A representative of the group said, "The pavilion will have a holographic image of you, inviting people to join you in the journey of discovering Jesus."

Whether this pavilion will ever take place remains to be seen, but picturing myself as a holographic image intrigued me. My mind recalled Star Trek spaceships, where people were beamed up or down on command—their light-filled particles assembling into recognizable human forms. And then it struck me—you and I *are* holographic images—a unique assemblage of light-filled particles sent to deliver a message and an expression of God.

We are beamed here through the wombs of our mothers and will be beamed back up through the tombs of our fathers.

Jesus calls us to be the light of the world.

How are we using this time on this planet? To do good, do evil, or just gather dust?

Divine connection. I don't know about you, but I want to live this life, and leave this life, beaming light and love.

QUESTIONS

1. What do you hope to accomplish on this planet before you are beamed home?

2. Where do you see yourself as separate from God?

Dear Lord,

Thank you for my being and my beingness. Help me to use this gift of a life, and of a time, wisely, that all may see your Light in me and you may be glorified. Amen.

BE IN A
FUTURE STATE

FAITH IS THE SUBSTANCE OF THINGS HOPED FOR,
THE EVIDENCE OF THINGS NOT SEEN.
—HEBREWS 11:1

One of the principles that will change your life the most is that of vision—or of being in a future state as if it were already true. Jesus said, "I tell you . . . everything you ask and pray for, believe that you have it already, and it will be yours" (Mark 11:24 NJB).

Jesus came to demonstrate and teach transformation, and faith is the transformative power of the universe.

When Jesus becomes your Coach, you will be asked to see what isn't yet seen, to move onto a bridge that doesn't seem to be there, to describe the taste of honey when you're swallowing tears.

I was privileged to actually visit the holy site of Lourdes in France. The story is that there a young girl saw the Virgin Mary, who asked her to dig in the dirt. The girl dug and dug while the villagers mocked her, for she was digging in a pigsty. Day after day the young girl returned to dig. Suddenly her fingers felt dampness in the soil. The dirt turned to mud, the mud turned to water, and a spring was born—a spring that brought forth healing waters—a spring called Lourdes. This young girl believed in the stream, even though at the time it was spoken of to her, it wasn't there.

A young boy was given a dream. He saw his brothers bowing down to him, and there were sheaves of wheat everywhere. He awakened in a state of wonder and shared the dream with his older brothers. "What, shall we bow down to you?" they said before throwing him in a well. He was then sold as a slave and taken to a foreign land. Many years went by until one day, he was ruler of Egypt and all its wheat. His brothers came from home seeking food and, not suspecting that the man before them was their brother, bowed down. Joseph was given a vision that came true in God's perfect time.

Perhaps you've been given a vision—one that maybe you have despaired of ever coming true. No matter what the circumstances, God sees clearly the real you—the healed you—the powerful you—the prosperous you—the person you dream to be—the person you *really* are, prospering in that abundant life.

Now your job is to believe it.

QUESTIONS

1. Do you have a dream or a vision that you've given up on?

2. What if it was still true—could be true—in God's eyes?

3. Why would faith be an ingredient of vision?

4. What are you doing to nurture your faith, or perhaps more important, where are you digging and why?

Dear Lord,
Help me get my fingernails dirty in the places where you tell me to dig. Amen.

UNDERSTAND
THE POWER OF
PRESENCE

I AM WITH YOU ALWAYS.
—MATTHEW 28:20 (NKJV)

Perhaps you have experienced meeting or being with a person of presence. He or she can walk into a room, and suddenly the attention and energy shift. It's not about physical appearance *per se*, but how this person holds himself or herself in the space.

Somehow the person conveys the presence of majesty

and might, no matter what the situation. And when we are in that presence, somehow we are transformed.

Jesus came to demonstrate the presence of God.

Presence means "bearing, or how one holds one's personality in a space."

For instance, my sister, Kathy, is one of the kindest and funniest people on the planet. She can simply say the words *World Wide Web* with a hint of a raised eyebrow and transform me into giggles. An innocence and subtlety about her turn me into being funnier, too. She and I were almost thrown out of a restaurant once when discussing our own funerals because we started laughing so hard, we were almost convulsing. My sister only has to say a word, and the laughter begins to spring up in me.

There is something about my sister's *presence* that makes me that way. Just thinking about her as I write this, I can feel little bubbles of laughter starting to come up through my veins. It makes me want to be with her again and again.

Likewise, I recall the presence of my friend Susanna Palomares. Susanna is the essence of grace and a lover of all things living. She took me once to the Everglades, "to help me overcome my fear of swamps and alligators," she said.

We walked to the edge of a particular marsh and stood there in silence as the sun began to set. A crane that had been curved like a statue suddenly stretched its wings and began to rise into the sky. We could hear the whoosh of its wings as it ascended. I remember Susanna standing only one step behind me. Together we stood in awe—watching a magnificent creature display its "wingedness." Not a word was spoken between us, but I felt as if I'd been in the presence of God. I was reminded of a passage from the book of Proverbs: "When he fixed the heavens firm, I was there" (8:27 NJB).

Presence in times of beauty reminds me of God.

Presence in times of sorrow reminds me of God.

Sam Faraone is a chaplain with the El Paso Police Department. When I asked him why he volunteered to meet people in times of great trauma and stress, he said simply, "Because I think it is something Jesus would do." When Sam and I worked together to determine his mission statement, all his desire boiled down to these few words: "My mission is to establish the presence of God."

I first met Sam when he came with the police to inform our family that a relative had killed himself. In the shock and grief and questioning of that horrible tragedy, Sam was there, sometimes hugging us, sometimes sitting silently, sometimes helping us clean up the blood. How very grateful we all were for the presence of a chaplain named Sam Faraone. It wasn't what he said that day that made the difference for all of us; it was that he was there.

In Psalm 17 King David wrote about his yearning to feel God's presence. I think about this verse often, for it translates the desire not to have a God who is at our beck and call, doing things for us, but to have a God that we get to simply "be with" and enjoy:

> For me the reward of virtue
> is to see your face—
> and to gaze my fill
> on your likeness. (v. 15, paraphrased)

All of scripture, really, represents a yearning for the presence of God. Jesus calls us to fall deeper and deeper into that Be-ing of God. For in that presence, we can indeed be wonder-full.

QUESTIONS

1. Whose presence do you most enjoy?

2. What qualities about that person (or those persons) actually transform you?

3. What would it mean if you knew you could always be in God's presence?

Dear Lord,
Help me to stop and remember that you are indeed everywhere—especially right here with me—in this very moment. Amen.

HAVE A

SAFE

SPACE

I GO TO PREPARE A PLACE FOR YOU.
—JOHN 14:2

When I first began contemplating Jesus as a motivator of people as well as the Son of God, I was intrigued by how he was able to get people to be so open with him. I have often tried to imagine standing beside him as he spoke to the woman at the well or summoned the fishermen to drop their nets and follow him. He had no pull with them that was based on power, prestige, celebrity, or money. He offered them nothing, except a chance to be who they fully could be and to do something great.

I am convinced that the reason the people followed him, and his chosen few ultimately were willing to die for him, was that he offered them a safe space. Not "safe" in terms of no danger coming to them. In fact, he warned that they would sacrifice many comforts and perhaps their lives if they followed him.

What he offered was a space that was safe for them to be who they truly were and could be. The space he offered them was not a building or a church, but a relationship of unconditional positive regard.

Somehow, through his words and his deeds, and the way he beheld them, they understood that all their weaknesses and past failures did not matter to him. He was not interested in their past—he was all about their future.

People who have attended our Path Training Seminars have often commented on how quickly the people in the group seem to open up to one another. Strangers, many from different countries, are willing to reveal their hearts and souls and shadows and fears in a short period of time. Many factors contribute to this phenomenon. The number one factor is the presence of God. "Where two or three are gathered together in my name, there am I in the midst of them," promised Jesus (Matt. 18:20), and we take him at his word.

Another way we make the space safe is through saturation prayer—before, during, and after the meeting, people are praying for the participants. We also don't allow "cross talking" while someone is speaking. Whoever is speaking must have the full attention of everyone in the room as a means of respect and focus. Everyone is there for a positive purpose, and that also comes through. There is a tone established from day one that says, "We are here to listen, learn, and love one another into fullness."

People cannot perform in an atmosphere of criticism or fear. Oh, they might be able to do so for a while, but in the end they will shut down, resist, rebel, or resign.

In order to coach and be coached effectively, both parties in the transaction need to establish a sense of safety and trust. This is done through a variety of ways. In the train-the-trainer sessions with our Path facilitators I share that there are three main requirements in order to help people's souls "emerge." One is that you must have only a positive intention in mind, free of ego constraints, considerations, and agendas. The second is that you must be willing to ask the difficult questions. And the third is that you must be unwilling to leave until the questions are answered. A psychological embrace, if you will, takes place. With the eyes looking forward, deep into the soul, and the arms lovingly held to form a safe circle, souls will emerge. I have seen it happen again and again.

Jesus saw it, and created it, daily. People want to blossom

and bloom. People want to do their best. People want to be creative and expressive and loved for who they are. But it takes someone to consciously create the space so that this can happen.

The staff at a hospital I work with commissioned a Patient Journey to determine how they could improve customer service. They wanted to observe what their service was like through the customers' eyes, which in this case were patients and their families. One of the things this detailed report revealed was that patients did not feel they had a space of their own. Their rooms were not their rooms, but merely holding places where they, the patients, would be prodded, interrupted, charted, awakened, and disturbed according to the timing and needs of the medical staff.

Patients also felt that their rooms looked alike. Their sense of individuality and their dignity were constantly being challenged by the established medical protocols of how things have always been done in hospitals. That is changing.

Soon, patients at this hospital will have a sense of ownership around their rooms. Doctors and nurses will knock before entering and try to arrange their schedules around the patients' needs, rather than vice versa. Patients who need to be in the hospital for longer than a five-day stay will be allowed to hang their own artwork on the walls—or artwork that is provided to them from an "art cart" furnished by the local museum of art. These are just a few of the small and big ways that hospital staff and executives are working to help patients heal in a space that is more emotionally sound than before.

Jesus created a safe space for people in many ways. He did it by defending his staff from criticism by the scribes and the Pharisees. He did it by defending the woman who washed his feet with her hair. He did it by telling the woman caught in adultery that all her accusers were gone now, and neither did he accuse her.

He did it by inviting the thief on the cross to come home with him that very day, even as both of them hung there dying. Jesus was able to look across at a man who was willing to admit his ignorance, and welcome that soul into paradise.

If only we could do the same. Yet all too often our homes, our schools, our workplaces are not safe emotionally. We have bullies in schools who intimidate and belittle and ignore those who are different from them. We have workplaces where bosses routinely yell and intimidate and threaten in order to get their way. We have homes where women and children cower when Daddy walks in the door, never knowing what mood he will be in. We have daughters who are ignored or belittled by their mothers, or molested by their uncles or stepfathers. The list could go on and on—and does.

But we have the ability to create a safe haven for others, just through the way we behold them. We can create an island of security for them, just by showing respect. By listening. By giving them time to formulate their words and ideas, and not getting up and leaving because it is taking too long.

When people feel safe, amazing things begin to happen. Why, sometimes, they even get up and walk.

Jesus created a safe space.

QUESTIONS

1. Where is your "safe" space?

2. Where do you not feel safe?

3. When have you felt the safest?

4. Why is a sense of safety essential for the soul to emerge?

Dear Lord,
You are my Rock, my Salvation, my Safety Net. I come to you and know that I am loved, no matter what. I come to you and know that you see all my failings and shortcomings, yet you love me anyway. I come to you praying that I will see what you see in me, and believe, and know, and grow into the person you created in such deep love and wonder. Amen.

KNOW THAT HE

IS ALWAYS REACHING

TOWARD YOU

YAHWEH CALLED ME WHEN I WAS IN THE WOMB,
BEFORE MY BIRTH HE HAD PRONOUNCED MY NAME.
—ISAIAH 49:1 (NJB)

Author Gregg Braden tells a wonderful story about a man
and the birth of his son. Gregg had happened to meet this
man and his family at a lovely seaside restaurant. As they
were waiting for their order, the two of them began con-
versing. After Gregg acknowledged the beauty of the man's

family, the man began to recount the difficulties and miracles of his youngest son's birth, whose name was Joshua.

It seems that Joshua's home birth was progressing normally until suddenly the baby stopped coming through the birth canal. His father, a trained paramedic, surmised that the baby's shoulder had gotten wedged against his mother's tailbone. The man reached inside his wife, found the tailbone, and moved his hand upward, just enough to feel his son's shoulder blade lodged up against the bone. He said to Gregg, "The most amazing thing happened." Just as the father was about to shift the infant's shoulder, he felt the baby grow still for a moment, as if uncertain at what he had just felt. Then within seconds the baby's tiny fingers closed confidently around his father's hand, and the father was able to successfully pull his son through the birth canal. The image of the unborn baby actually gripping his father's fingers, trusting him to bring him out safely, brought tears to my eyes.

I was blessed to be able to visit the Sistine Chapel in Italy with my mother. Having long seen the image of God reaching out to Adam in the creation scene, I was eager to view it with my own eyes. Yet that image is one of good-bye. God is telling Adam: "You are going to a new world now—on your own." In contrast, the image that Christ brings is one of "Hello . . . and . . . welcome to a whole new world."

Scripture tells us that even the earth is groaning in labor. We are constantly moving into new areas of being, thinking, and experiencing. How wonderful to know that even when you get stuck, there is a hand reaching out to you . . . eager and yearning to bring you into a whole new world.

Jesus is reaching out to you.

QUESTIONS

1. Do you feel stuck in your life right now?

2. Do you feel that you need to move?

3. What would it be like to realize that Jesus is reaching out to you right now?

Dear Lord,
Thank you for reaching into my messy, stuck situation and working to set me free. Help me trust you enough to place my tiny hand in yours. Amen.

EXPERIENCE

AMAZEMENT

THE MOST EXQUISITE FRUITS ARE AT OUR DOORS;
THE NEW AS WELL AS THE OLD, I HAVE STORED
THEM FOR YOU, MY LOVE.
—SONG OF SONGS 7:14 (NJB)

A friend of mine is a true romantic. To propose to his fiancée, he planned a ten-mile hike into the depths of the Grand Canyon. There, in front of Havasu Falls, he knelt and asked her to marry him. On the way there they encountered a man who was packing his way out. He asked if they had seen the Falls yet. When they replied that they hadn't, he opened his eyes wider and said in a thick German accent, "It is amazement!" They delighted in his word choice, for it truly spoke the meaning of the scene they were about to behold.

One day I went in to take a shower in my tiled bathroom in El Paso, Texas, and discovered a tiny, white, almost translucent gecko sitting on the shower floor. I could literally see his heart beating and his lungs taking in large gulps of air as he surveyed this new surrounding. Apparently he had come up through the drain because the shower was fully enclosed. I wondered how long he had been standing there, contemplating with awe this new world. I wondered what his original home looked like, existing somewhere in the water or sewer line. I doubt he knew that his route would bring him to this place of space and light. It made me think of how it might be when I enter heaven.

I carefully gathered him up and released him into my garden that has a continually running fountain and nice, damp flower beds. I am certain that the lives we live here will be like sewer lines and drain pipes compared to the garden of love we will be brought into.

My friend and pastor Dr. Tim Walker in Grapevine, Texas, shared that death must be like birth. Embryos in the womb know only darkness and rocking and silence, and enter this world reluctantly, crying in protest with their first breath. Yet when their eyes are opened, they encounter "amazement."

Life lived in the spirit, and in the presence of Jesus, is one of continually unfolding amazement. Miracles surround us daily if only we have eyes to see. Jesus will give you a new pair of eyes.

QUESTIONS

1. When have you entered into a state of amazement?

2. What was happening?

3. Describe a time when you saw something for the first time with new eyes. What was it? How did it feel?

Dear Lord,
Help me walk in a state of grateful amazement at all you have done for me. Amen.

BECOME THE
MESSAGE

DON'T THINK YOU HAVE TO PUT ON A
FUND-RAISING CAMPAIGN BEFORE YOU
START. YOU DON'T NEED A LOT OF
EQUIPMENT. *YOU* ARE THE EQUIPMENT.
—MATTHEW 10:9–10 (*THE MESSAGE*)

Roger Ailes became famous as a media consultant not only to the stars, but also to numerous political figures. Perhaps the most famous of his clients was President Ronald Reagan.

Roger was called in to consult with the president in preparation for his debates. In the first presidential debate,

Reagan had gone up against his opponent, Walter Mondale, who had appeared more at ease and more comfortable with statistics than the president was. Frankly the staff at the White House was worried.

People were afraid to say it, but everyone knew the truth. If the president appeared too old or out of touch with his constituents, he would lose the election. Thus there was a lot of pressure on both President Reagan and Roger Ailes when the two met.

For the first practice session, Roger merely watched the mock debates and took notes. People who were brought in specifically to be Reagan's opponents were trying to outfox and outmaneuver him at every turn—firing questions and comments and innuendos in order to prepare the president for any eventuality. They were especially trying to challenge him about facts and statistics since those areas had seemed to be his weaker points in the last debate. Roger could tell that Reagan was getting tired, frustrated, and agitated by the exercises. No matter how many times they brought him around to try to tackle the facts again, Reagan seemed to be flubbing his lines.

Finally Roger told everyone to leave—the staffers, the mock opponents, the sound people, everyone. He sat down with the president and began to reassure him. He said, "Mr. President, the people didn't elect you because of your ability to memorize statistics. They elected you because of who you are. They love your character and your sense of humor, and that is what they need to be reminded of. Don't let anyone get up there and fluster you. Just be yourself, and say what comes naturally."

The president nodded and smiled, suddenly more at ease with the situation.

When the second debate came around, the president seemed in a much better mood. Although he had certainly heard the doomsayers predict that he would go down in this second round as being too old and out of touch, he seemed unconcerned. In fact, when his opponent dared to bring up the issue of age, Reagan smiled and replied, "I have determined not to let the age and the relative inexperience of my opponent become an issue in this campaign." Everyone suddenly burst into laughter—the moderator, the reporters, and the audience. Even his opponent couldn't help stifling a laugh as the wisdom and good humor of the man Ronald Reagan shone forth.

It was a slam dunk for the president. The age issue never really came up again, either in the debate or in the election. Whenever it did surface in discussions, the president's humorous and good-natured one-liner was quoted, reminding people who this man really was. Reagan sailed into a second term

Jesus became very clear that he was God's Word made flesh. He said, "I am the way, the truth, and the life" (John 14:6). He said, "I am the good shepherd" (John 10:14). He said, "Whoever has seen me has seen the Father" (John 14:9

NRSV). He knew that he was God, here on earth, and he never wavered in that understanding, however difficult it made his life and his choices.

Somehow we all must be made to understand that through the miracle of spiritual transformation in Christ, we, too, become the message. No matter what words we say or how we act, it is our deeds and our being that people will remember.

Perhaps Pilate said it all when he declared, "Behold the Man!" (John 19:5 NKJV). With those words he was saying, "Look at him, and you will see everything that he is—without pretense, without artifice, without shame."

Too many of us are trying to be like, look like, or sound like someone else. Advertisers promoting specific brands tell us how to dress, what to eat, what to buy, what to watch, what to listen to.

Yet God is calling each of us to find, and live, his or her authentic voice. If only we could be who we *truly* are, this world would be changed in an instant.

You and I are the message. You are God's thoughts, God's hopes, God's dreams, God's passions, with skin on.

Perhaps you may be like many of the biblical heroes who tried to convince God that he had the wrong person for the job.

You don't want me to preach, God—I am a man of unclean lips. You don't want me to lead the people, God— I stutter. Isaiah. Moses. We love and remember and cherish their names because somehow they came to realize that, despite their fears and shortcomings, they were the message and the voice of God in their situation. It is no different today for you and for me.

Jesus knew that he was the message.

And so are you.

QUESTIONS

1. Where and how are you trying to be someone else?

2. If someone looked not at the words, but at the theme of your life, what would it be?

3. How would your life change if you realized that you are God's message in your very world?

Dear Lord,

Wow! You have stunned me. You have exalted me. You have shocked me. You have instilled in me the growing sense of wonder and fear and realization that in this world, in this time, in this place, I am your message and your messenger. Help me stay true to the note that you created me to be. Amen.

LOOK AT THE WORLD
THROUGH NEW EYES

THE LITTLE GIRL IS NOT DEAD;
SHE IS ASLEEP.
—MATTHEW 9:24 (NJB)

Science now knows that as our perception of an object changes, its behavior will change. This principle even has a name: the Heisenberg Uncertainty Principle. It basically means that our expectations and beliefs shape behaviors. It also means that "as you believe, you shall receive."

One of the most amazing gifts that Jesus, your Life Coach, will bring you is that of a new perspective. A reading of any of the parables in the Gospels reveals his astonishing way of looking at the world through new eyes:

+ "If you have faith, even as a mustard seed, you could move this mountain."

+ "You could tear down this temple, and in three days I would raise it again."

+ "If you believe in me, and ask in my name, nothing shall be impossible to you."

I often picture little cartoonlike bubbles over the people's heads who were trying to make sense of what he was saying. The word that pops up for me most often is the three-letter word *Huh?* "What is this man saying? To give away our cloaks to those who have wronged us? To turn a cheek to those who would slap us? To walk an extra mile with someone who is pressing us into slavery? Is this person crazy?"

In the world's eyes, he was. But his kingdom is not of this world, and now, neither is yours.

The Sunday school class I was attending in Phoenix began to discuss a recent tragedy in the news. The space shuttle with seven astronauts had disintegrated on re-entry eerily descending in a stream of flames across a clear blue sky. We had watched it on the news just the day before, and we were all struggling to come to terms with the sudden loss of seven bright, eager, intelligent adventurers—some of our very finest.

A white-haired man named Ed said something I will never forget. He leaned forward and said, "It is at times like this that eternity breaks through." There was a long silence in the room as his words seeped into our hearts.

When events beyond our control and our ability to comprehend take place, these are the moments when eternity breaks through.

Jesus said, "There is a time and place when no tear will ever fall again, nor any sorrow be remembered. I have come from that place to remind you that this, too, is where you come from, and where I shall lead you home."

One evening at an event, I stood behind a giant screen, waiting to be called up on stage. My escort stood faithfully beside me, his hand gently resting on my arm. I could hear people singing on the other side, but I could not see their faces. If I looked up at the screen in front of me, I could vaguely make out what the words were, although they all read backward.

At the pre-agreed-upon moment the music changed, the lights came up, and I heard my name. As the applause began to build, he whispered, "I know you'll do great."

I went up the stairs, turned, and suddenly I could clearly read the words as well as behold the people's faces in front of me.

Before I had been behind the screen, but now I could see face-to-face.

Before I had stood in a darkened hallway, but now light flooded over me.

Jesus, my Coach, had brought me here.

Jesus will give you, too, a whole new perspective as he takes you from behind the screen.

QUESTIONS

1. What screen are you standing behind? Is it doubt or fear?

2. Imagine coming around the other side of that and finding only joy. Who is holding your hand as you wait in darkness?

Dear Lord,
Take my hand and lead me into Your light. Amen.

HAVE

UNBOUNDED

JOY

YOU WILL TEACH ME THE PATH OF LIFE,
UNBOUNDED JOY IN YOUR PRESENCE.
—PSALM 16:11 (NJB)

King David expressed a mystical joy when he wrote,

> My heart rejoices, my soul delights,
> my body too will rest secure,
> for you will not abandon me to Sheol . . .

You will teach me the path of life,
unbounded joy in your presence,
at your right hand delight for ever.
(Ps. 16:9–11 NJB)

There is a joy to be had in a personal relationship with
God that the "regular" world often cannot understand. We
are told in the book of Acts that when the Holy Spirit fell
on the group of apostles gathered there, they all began to
speak in languages they didn't understand. When they
poured out of the Upper Room and into the city streets,
they were so ludicrously happy that the people thought
they were drunk (Acts 2).

Jesus himself was accused of being a joyous winebibber.
In his prayers he asked constantly that our joy might be full.

Encountering God and surrendering to him leave you
breathless, in an altered state often too beautiful to describe.
One ancient poet wrote: "I am like an ant stumbled into a
granary, struggling to carry out a grain far larger than I, feeling ludicrously happy."

My yellow Labrador Chula breaks into circles of joy
when I return from a trip (even if it is to the grocery store).
She tucks her tail between her legs and lays her ears back
and takes off running through the yard at full speed—
careening around fence posts and wagon wheels—needing
to be in motion to express the ecstasy that has taken over
her body. A simple tail wag won't do it. She has to run.

My godson is the same way. One time I went to visit him when he was three years old after not having seen him for a period of six weeks. I walked in the door, and he looked up at me and screamed, then started running laps through the house as fast as his little legs would carry him. He circled past me and his laughing mom and then headed off down the hallway again, grinning up at me each time he passed. That day he ran twenty-two circles through the house, so glad he was to see me. Heart connections, not based on words. Just the simple joy of feeling *one.*

This is the way Jesus feels about you. Angels shout; the party hats come out; the finest wine is opened and poured. The joy of union and reunion is what this Coach wants for you.

When Jesus is your Coach, you feel unbounded joy, and begin to recognize the joy he feels for *you.*

QUESTIONS

1. When in your life have you been ecstatically happy?

2. What if you could experience this feeling consistently?

3. What is the difference between joy and achievement?

4. You were created in joy, and to joy you will return. Meanwhile, joy on earth is available to you in ways that pass all human understanding. Are you open to it?

Dear Lord,

Help me awaken to your joy—the joy you have in me and for me. In you is all my desire and my reward. Amen.

PAINT WHAT
YOU LOVE

AND TO ONE HE GAVE FIVE TALENTS, TO
ANOTHER TWO, AND TO ANOTHER ONE, TO EACH
ACCORDING TO HIS OWN ABILITY.
—MATTHEW 25:15 (NKJV)

A quote card that I purchased at the Georgia O'Keeffe museum in Santa Fe, New Mexico, is in my briefcase, so I have it handy at all times. It is a statement the artist made in reference to her unending love affair with New Mexico. She said, "It belongs to me. God told me if I painted it often enough I could have it." We are artists in our own way—

attempting to express ourselves on the canvas of our daily lives. The sad thing is that so often we miss our own art because we do not step back and observe where the brush strokes are going.

My mother is a constant source of joy and surprise to me. Recently she took the initiative to form her own art group. It is called LWAOS, which stands for Loose Women Artists of Sedona. The group meets once a week on Wednesdays in the clubhouse from nine in the morning until two in the afternoon.

Each week one of them assigns an experimental art form that all must participate in. The only goal of the group is to stay loose and have fun. When I called Mom and asked her what the group came up with this week, she said, "We did paintings that you could hang from any angle—upside down or sideways. The whole purpose was not about perspective, but balance and color." Who knows what she and her group are going to come up with next?

Mom is eighty-two years old and yet only ten—having a blast creating her own second childhood. She is doing what she loves.

My friend and coworker Marty Blubaugh called me yesterday, recounting his trip to Washington, D.C., on my behalf. Marty shared with me that on the plane ride back, he sat next to a woman who works at a major military supplier, making a lot of money, yet somehow hating her job. Marty explained to her what we were doing with teens and how my book, *The Path*, had helped him get more clear about his gifts and calling as well. When she got off the plane, she turned to him and said, "I have hope now. I just didn't want to spend the next half of my life doing a job that I hate, even if there is a lot of money involved." Marty and I and all our Path facilitators are passionate about people being able to paint what they love and make a living at it.

Interestingly enough, I was perusing my journal this morning and came across a poem I wrote about Marty's seven-year-old son, Scotty:

Scotty

I was unprepared for his beauty—
front tooth missing—the gap centered
under large dancing eyes
flecked with gold.
His hair lay upon his head
in a perfect circumference
of gold peach fuzz—
finely shorn
finishing in a cowlick off
the center of his forehead.
His little chest spread out under his tee shirt.
His skinny legs ended in tennis shoes,
one of them untied.
"What did you do today at school, Scott?"
asked his solemn father.

"Nothing much, Dad—hung out on the playground at lunch
and then ate *cupcakes!*" he shouted.
He lifted his face up to me—
seven years in forming—and laughed,
"Cupcakes, cupcakes—slap me silly,
but that is what I love the most."
And my heart flew into him
unprepared as it was
for his beauty.
4/15/01

Scotty was showing unending delight in *his* school subject of choice. I believe that each of us can be working in a cupcake mode . . . doing what we love most every day. In fact, this is my passion.

My challenge to you is to fill in this blank, imitating the cupcake verse of Scotty, listing the subject in life you most love.

"_____,_____, slap me silly, but that is what I love the most."

Yours might read: "Gardening, gardening, slap me silly, but that is what I love the most." Could you make a living by gardening? Many people do.

Or yours might read: "Building, building, slap me silly, but that is what I love the most." Can you make a living building things? Many people do.

Now imagine if you could make a living doing every day what you most love to do. Be like Georgia O'Keeffe. Understand that if you paint it often enough, God will give it to you.

Jesus left the carpentry shop of his father to head out into the wilderness, teaching, healing, and preaching, urging us to come out of our boxes and reach for the sky.

Jesus painted what he loved, and he challenges us to do the same.

QUESTIONS

1. If someone were to interpret your brush strokes today, what would your painting portray?

2. Why did Georgia O'Keeffe think that God would give her something if she painted it enough? What did she mean by that?

Dear Lord,
Help me paint what is loved, and lovable, in your eyes. Help me also understand that somehow, I am your great masterpiece, and that doing what I love the most gives pleasure to you, my Creator. Amen.

THOUGHTS AND A PRAYER

I learned yesterday that everyone loses twenty-one grams when they die. Whether the body is young or old, heavy or thin, something ineffable leaves it that weighs only as much as a hummingbird.

Perhaps this is what the human soul weighs, or the breath that circulates through our lungs day in, day out—from our first great gulp of air to our last soft sigh.

This is the part of you that Jesus seeks—not the weight of your accomplishments or the heft of your bank account—not even (dare I say it?) the list of your good deeds.

Jesus is looking for the essence of you—the twenty-one grams granted at birth—the twenty-one grams that may ascend into heaven when you die.

Turn your breath to him now—whisper a first "yes," and then again and again a "yes"—and your life will turn imperceptibly, boldly, hugely toward the ultimate, greatest, happiest "You."

Amen and Amen.

EPILOGUE

Not long ago I had the privilege of assisting a group of officers at the United States Naval Academy in Annapolis, Maryland. My friend Claudia Coe initiated and led the meeting, where for three hours we helped some of the finest and brightest officers in the Navy develop their individual mission statements. All were in uniform. All are committed to serving their country. Their mission statements are varied and moving, and I've quoted a few of them here with the officers' permission:

> To inspire, drive, and accomplish justice.
> To sacrifice for, dream, and appreciate love.
> To explore, translate, and enlighten inner peace.
> To create, connect, and inspire others in humility.
> To brighten, create, and nurture wholeness.
> To support, safeguard, and worship trust.
> To motivate, envision, and encourage integrity.
> To inspire, dream, and surrender to wisdom.
> To educate, lead, and heal through spirited service.
> To inspire, mold, and motivate through integrity.
> To communicate, educate, and foster others through service.

Notice the simple beauty and power of the words they chose to represent who they are. How blessed I felt to be among such a fine group of people in such challenging times.

As I walked the marbled halls afterwards, I couldn't help but reflect on the need we have, now more than ever, to be clear about what we came here to do. The following day I flew to Washington, D. C., and met with congressional representatives in both the House and Senate to discuss funding for helping at-risk youth. I'm pleased to say we have been successful in our appeal for youth in three cities: El Paso, Indianapolis, and Tuscaloosa. These cities will be served in the next few years through our Path Community Services program and the YMCA. Hopefully by the time you read this there will be even more cities on the list.

Thanks to my friend and Path facilitator Amy Crumpton, just two months prior to the congressional meetings I had the opportunity to talk to the president and CEO of Wal-Mart, the world's largest company. There we received their blessing and pledges of support for our youth program.

After that meeting I came home and began cleaning out my garage to make room for expanding our offices for these new ventures. Dusty boxes revealed scattered notes I'd written—reminders of dreams I've had for the last twenty years . . . dreams about lifting up Jesus in new and exciting ways . . . dreams about helping people see how unique and special their gifts are and how cherished they are by God. My dusty dreams are coming true before my very eyes.

In one of my recent Path seminars there was a young man I shall call "Ken." He was only in his twenties and had been very quiet on the first day of our seminar. It seemed he was trying to get a feeling for what was happening. On the last day he stood up and began to speak. He said, "When I came here I was determined not to laugh or cry. I felt that as the youngest person here I didn't have anything to contribute, so I just kept quiet. But I can't keep quiet anymore.

"I never knew my father, and I am sorry about that. I was determined to make my mother proud of me, however, so I worked very hard at sports and at my studies in college. But I realize now that I always hung back a little bit. My friends wanted me to run for student body president, but I didn't, because I was afraid. My coach wanted me to try out for the professional sports teams, but I didn't, because I was afraid. And now I realize I have to do something to contribute, and it is this. When your coach tells you to 'Step up to the plate'—step up. From now on, I will."

I pray that when my Coach calls me to step up to the plate, I do.

And I pray the same for you.

—LAURIE BETH JONES

ABOUT THE AUTHOR

Laurie Beth Jones has written several national best-selling books, including *Jesus, CEO: Using Ancient Wisdom for Visionary Leadership, The Path: Creating Your Mission for Work and Life, Jesus in Blue Jeans, Jesus, Inc.,* and *Teach Your Team to Fish.* Her work has been featured in *Time, Business Week, CNN, Industry Week Magazine,* and *USA Today.*

After launching and running her own successful advertising agency for fifteen years, Laurie Beth Jones burst onto the national scene with *Jesus, CEO* a book that espoused bringing spiritual principles back into the business world. That book, and subsequent books that followed, spent more than thirteen months on the *Business Week* Bestseller List, and have been translated into twelve foreign languages, with worldwide sales of one million copies.

Using practical wisdom, bursts of humor, and reality-based thinking, Ms. Jones has become one of the world's leading consultants for businesses that want to take their work—and their workers—to unparalleled levels of performance, satisfaction, and success.

Her work has reached as high as the White House, the Pentagon, the halls of Congress and the Senate, as well as the depths of workers in the streets of Calcutta, Bosnia, and South Africa. Her Path for Teens Program has received the blessing and support of Wal-Mart, and her Path Training Program is currently in use in the character development program at the United States Naval Academy in Annapolis, Maryland, as well as in various training programs around the country. She has been called upon by billionaires and kings, pastors, students, housewives and prisoners to help discern their spiritual paths, and she lives out her mission daily, which is to "recognize, promote, and inspire the divine connection in myself and others."

For more information log on to
www.lauriebethjones.com.

ACKNOWLEDGMENTS

This book would not have come into being without the visionary efforts of Terry Barber, Victor Oliver, and Jonathan Merkh at Thomas Nelson. Their urging and encouragement helped keep me on the path to completion. I would like to thank Tami Simon, who helped form the original thought process around the title, as well as Jane Creswell, who stepped up with much appreciated research on executive coaching.

Other members of the team at Thomas Nelson who helped this project become real include: Kristen Lucas, Brecca Theele, Larry Ross & Associates, and the marketing team.

For my friends and Congressional leaders in Washington who provided support, encouragement, and endorsement for Path Community Services, a special thank you: John Waites, Wes Bizzell, Richard Reyes, Henry Bonilla, Julia Carson, Richard C. Shelby, Jeff Sessions, Artur Davis, Spencer Bachus, Dianne Feinstein, Barbara Boxer, Susan A. Davis, Duncan L. Hunter, Richard G. Lugar, Evan Bayh, Julia M. Carson, Dan Burton, Jeff Bingaman, Pete V. Domenici, Heather A. Wilson, Tom Udall, John Edwards,

Elizabeth Dole, Sue Myrick, Brad Miller, Bobby Etheridge, David E. Price, Kay Bailey Hutchison, John Cornyn, and Martin Frost.

Others I wish to thank include Dick Stenbakken, Greg Bunch, and Mike Regan. Ken and Margie Blanchard, Rick Warren, John Maxwell, Bill Pollard, Franklin Graham, Don Soderquist, David Miller, and Michael A. Volkema have continued to challenge me to higher and deeper walks with the Lord.

I am blessed to have a number of friends within the YMCA, including Gordon Echtenkamp, Norris Lineweaver, Michelle Goodrich, Roger Davies, Cynthia Flynn, Erik Daubert, Richard Colloto, and others.

To Doug Hawthorne, a leader who walks the talk, thank you for inspiration, encouragement, and support.

To Tom Coglin and Lee Scott, CEO and president of Wal-Mart, thank you for taking the time to make a difference in a big way for at-risk youth.

Path facilitators who continue to provide me with inspiration and support include: Bob Jewell, Amy Crumpton, Claudia Coe, Robin Chaddock, Gaye Lindfors, Charley Waldo, Debbie Haynes, Janine Finney, Kathy Marcil, Jacque Salamy, Vangie Chavez, Polly Anderson, Linda Miller, Tom Heck, and others who have graced my path this last year.

Ionna Morfessis has provided special encouragement in my daily walk, adding fire and light at every opportunity.

Captain Elizabeth Holmes, Captain Robert Schoultz, and Major William Collins at Annapolis, have blessed and inspired me with their leadership skills and passion for character development.

To my dedicated assistant, Rosario Muñoz, who makes my life flow so smoothly because of her behind-the-scenes work and love for people, thank you. I couldn't do this without you.

Thank you to my friends and colleagues at Communities in schools in El Paso. You are helping so many wonderful young people find their way. You inspire me with your courage and compassion: Robert Shaw, Robert Ramirez, Argelia Morales, Adreana Ramirez, Belinda Ortega, Brenda Torres, Amanda Saucedo, Isidro Frayre, Lauroselle Johnson, Tyrone Garner, Vangie Franco, Terry Randle, Martha Campos, Tina Quiñones, Brenda Trejo-Barri, Lauren Galos-Willia, and Arlene Lira.

To Shelly Buckner, who helped take the skeleton of an idea and turn it into a living, breathing entity for good— thank you. You are truly dedicated to God and growth.

To Marty Blubaugh, for laboring so patiently and diligently to help my arrows find their mark, thank you. You are a noble and worthy warrior.

A very special thanks to Jerry Mabe, Lee Ellis, and Sue Clark for their excellent leadership and assistance in helping take the Path Element Profile to the next level.

To Catherine Calhoun, my ongoing gift from God. You

always bathe me in laughter and loving words, even as you speak and seek the truth. I wouldn't be where I am without you.

To my sister, Kathy Lee Ivey and her family Ben, Ben Jr., and Tara; and my brother Joseph Jones and his wife Barbara Hanlon. Thank you for being the best siblings and supporters any person could have.

And to my mother, Irene Jones, who keeps me laughing as she paints what she loves. Thank you for living your life in joy.

OTHER COACHING TOOLS

Would you like Laurie Beth Jones as your personal coach? For information on her availability to coach you or your team, call Rosario Muñoz at (915) 541-6033, or contact us at **www.lauriebethjones.com**. Laurie Beth is also available for keynote speaking, teambuilding sessions, or leadership retreats.

NEW! PATH ELEMENTS PROFILE (PEP)™

In her book *The Path: Creating Your Mission for Work and Life*, Laurie Beth Jones introduced the concept of linking the elements of earth, water, wind, and fire to people's personality traits. Now you can go on-line to discover not only which elements you are most like (Earth, Water, Wind or Fire), but also how much of each element you are. This interactive tool is easy, fun, and can profoundly impact your understanding of your behaviors, as well as that of those around you. Jesus said he was Living Water. What are you? Log on to www.lauriebethjones.com.

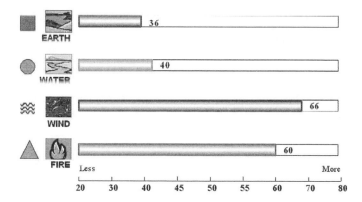

If you desire to learn how to help others get clear on their mission in life, or even help yourself become more clear, experiencing a Path Seminar may be just the hands-on, face-to-face, experiential process, and gift you need. Log on to our website for dates, times, and locations.

Path for Teens Program

This 30-week curriculum is ideal for parents, youth leaders, counselors and teachers who work with young people. Now being launched in multiple states, in partnership with schools, YMCAs, and other nonprofits, we are seeking partners to help raise up the next generation. Log on to **www.path4u.com** to learn more.

Path for Kids CD Activity Book, Children's Songs cassette, Kids Color the Songs

This CD rom offers numerous exercises and programs to help kids learn more about their gifts, talents, and their ability to serve others. We also have a Children Songs and coloring book available for the little ones.

Jesus, CEO

Jesus, CEO: Using Ancient Wisdom for Visionary Leadership is a practical, step-by-step guide to communicating with and motivating people. It is based on the self-mastery, action, and relationship skills that Jesus used to train and motivate his team. It can be applied to any business, service, or endeavor that depends on more than one person to accomplish a goal, and can be implemented by anyone who dares.

This book launched it all with a bold assertion that Jesus of Nazareth was and is the ultimate Chief Executive Officer. Hitting the *Business Week* Bestseller list immediately upon publication, it has since been translated into thirteen foreign languages, and has been featured in *Time* magazine, *Business Week, Industry Week,* and *USA Today,* as well as on CNN and the BBC. Short chapters and simple questions spawned study groups worldwide.

The Path

In a world in which we are daily forced to make decisions that lead us either closer to or further from our goals, no tool is as valuable in providing direction as a mission statement—a brief, succinct, and focused statement of purpose that can be used to initiate, evaluate, and refine all of life's activities. A carefully thought out mission statement acts as both a harness and a sword—harnessing you to what is true about your life, and cutting away all that is false.

In *The Path*, Laurie Beth Jones provides inspiring and practical advice to lead readers through every step of both defining and fulfilling a mission. Jones offers clear, step-by-step guidance that can make writing a mission statement take a matter of hours rather than months or years.

The Path Training Seminars and Path for Teens Program are based on this book.

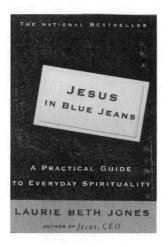

Jesus in Blue Jeans

Jesus in Blue Jeans is the conclusion to Laurie Beth Jones's trilogy, which began with her nationally bestselling books, *Jesus, CEO* and *The Path*. In this book, Laurie turns from the business world to everyday existence and reveals numerous ways of attaining spirituality and grace in our personal lives through the teachings of Jesus.

Following the example of Jesus—a "CEO" who took a disorganized "staff" of twelve and built a thriving enterprise—Laurie Beth Jones details a simple, profound, fresh, and often humor-filled approach to motivating and managing others.

LAURIE BETH JONES
AUTHOR OF JESUS, CEO

Jesus,

Entrepreneur

ORIGINALLY PUBLISHED AS JESUS, INC.

USING ANCIENT WISDOM TO
LAUNCH AND LIVE YOUR DREAMS

Jesus Entrepreneur

One of the biggest workplace trends of the last few years has been the hunger for meaning and spirituality among people who once pursued their careers solely for money and prestige. Whether they work independently, for small businesses, or for major corporations, millions of Americans are now determined to use their talents to benefit the world as well as themselves. Consultant and bestselling author Laurie Beth Jones calls these people "spiritreneurs" because they fully bring their souls into their workplaces, usually with considerable initiative and risk. She also suggests that Jesus was the ultimate spiritreneur, because he gave up a comfortable living as a carpenter to pursue a new line of work that would really affect human lives.

With *Jesus Entrepreneur* Jones shows how we can all follow his example to pursue work that supports our deepest spiritual and personal beliefs. In addition to tales from the Bible, she also shares anecdotes from her own life, including real-world stories from the best and worst workplace situations she has encountered.

Teach Your Team To Fish

When Jesus called out to the fishermen, "Follow me, and I will make you fishers of men," He was about to transform each one of those recruits from someone who worked only for a daily paycheck to someone who was part of a larger team, working for eternity. As a teambuilder, you have been given perhaps the most challenging and rewarding work on earth today, which is teaching human beings to think and act like a team.

In *Teach Your Team To Fish* Laurie Beth Jones presents 47 clear principles designed to help you to excite, ground, transform and release your team, just as Jesus did.

My personal mission and vision is to create, nurture, and sustain Maximum Positive Impact in the Seven Pillars of Society, which are:

Business, Education, Healthcare, Faith and Service Organizations, the Government, the Mass Media, and the Disenfranchised.

My friends and associates and I will prayerfully do this by influencing though leaders in each of the Seven Pillars with this principle: Jesus of Nazareth is the ultimate role model for leadership and decision making in every aspect of life. Come join us in this work. Log onto our Website at www.lauriebethjones.com.

Blessings to you!
Laurie Beth Jones